Holding Space

A Guide to Supporting Others While Remembering to Take Care of Yourself First

Amanda Dobra Hope

For those who need a reminder to love, honor, and care for themselves first before attempting to assist others — these words were given to me for you.

Table of Contents

Introduction 1

Preface-Definition of Terms 5

A Personal Journey Through the Life of a Spaceholder

The Beginning of the Journey to Greater Self-Awareness......................11

Allowing Yourself to Be Uncomfortable

Spiritual Connections/Considerations in Holding Space......................17

The Role of Intuition in Spaceholding

How Your Higher Power and Ethereal Team Hold Space for You

Personal Growth and Self-Care 23

Why You Should Always Take Care of Yourself First

Taking Space for Yourself: Practical Tools for "How" to Take Care of Yourself First

Honoring Yourself as a Master Holder of Space

How to Use Your Gifts to Your Advantage

Understanding and Directing Your Energy and Setting Energetic Boundaries

The Spaceholder in Personal Relationships 43

Why Others Might Resist You

Spaceholding to Protect Yourself and Your Relationships When Others are Out of Alignment, Unbalanced, or Angry

Holding Space in Relationships Until They "Come Around Again"

Tools for How to Cope When Someone "Needs Their Space"

Holding Space for Friends or Family Members When They Need to Fall in Order to Get Back Up On Their Own

Holding Space for Yourself and Others in Order to Affect "Real Change"

Being Honest With Yourself About When and How Much Space You Can Hold for a Partner

Holding Space When a Decision Needs to Be Made-"Keeping the Conversation Open"

Being Present, "Keeping Things on Track," and Shifting--Performing the Job of Spaceholder in Personal Relationships

Holding Space for the Dreams of Others

Holding Space for Someone to Become Who They Really Are

"Being There" for People When Times are Tough

In the Creation Process 71

Being in the Bubble- Staying Focused

Holding Space for Your Dreams

Holding Space to Allow Your Talents, Passions, and Dreams to Show Themselves to You

Manifesting Your Destiny 77

Holding Space for Love, Money, or Anything Else You Wish to Manifest to Come to You (Using the Law of Attraction in Spaceholding)

Working Smarter and Not Harder- Getting Out of Your Own Way

Holding Space for Your Body, Mind, and Spirit, After You Take a Big Step Forward (The Healing Crisis)

Holding Space for Yourself and Keeping Yourself Comfortable: While You Wait, When You're Weary, or When You're 'Almost There'

Letting Go

Spaceholding as a Profession 89

Being Present, "Keeping Things on Track," and Shifting -As a Professional Spaceholder

Ceremonies/Rituals/Rites of Passage and Holding Space

Counselors/Therapists/Life Coaches/Clergy

The "Wisdom Keepers" and the "Activists"

If You Become a Parent 101

Holding Space for Children is Different than Holding Space for Adults

How Your Spaceholding Practices Can Affect the World 107

Making Yourself a Channel for Love and Peace- "Be-ing" Love

Becoming the Best Spaceholder That You Can Be

Holding Space for All Humanity Through Looking at Our Individual and Collective Shadows

Holding Space for Growth and Change in Romantic Partnerships and Friendships, and How This Can Affect the Healing of the Entire Planet

Conclusion 117

Why Holding Space is Important to Transforming the World

Introduction

Are you a *spaceholder*? Do you even know what that means, or who or what it describes?

I had no idea that was one of my major earthly jobs and talents until a few years ago. Turns out I was doing (well, mostly *being*) many things related to spaceholding and always had been, it's just that the nomenclature of what I was doing hadn't gone mainstream yet.

The art of spaceholding is yet undefined. Despite the fact that it is something so many of us do every day and that it requires an enormous amount of energy, spaceholding gets little attention. I would like to alleviate that issue by defining it in depth throughout this book. Chances are that you are already holding space in many ways for yourself, for others around you, and even for situations in which you probably just don't realize that you are doing it.

So what is a spaceholder?

A spaceholder is a person who holds an energetic container for themselves, others, or a situation, while allowing organically whatever needs to arise out of that situation for the highest good of the person or situation. It is a state of *allowing*. Spaceholding can be used in both personal and professional settings. The purpose of this book is to both define and explain what spaceholding is, as well as to point out where you are already holding space in your life so you can learn to honor, value, and take care of yourself as you provide this very important service for yourself and for those that you affect.

Spaceholding is used in every type of relationship, your relationships with other people, as well as your relationships with situations, projects, discussions, or anything else. Spaceholding can be intentional, or it can naturally and spontaneously happen. You hold space when you allow yourself or someone else to fully experience all of their feelings (whether they are messy or uncomfortable, or pleasurable), when you wait for the proper timing to take action on something, or when you let yourself or someone else talk or have emotions without reacting or trying to fix or solve anything. You can also hold space when you're just not sure of what to do next and therefore, you just go about your everyday tasks while you keep the idea on the back burner in your awareness but not actively working on a solution for it.

Spaceholding can also be done professionally. Some easy examples of where I myself am a professional spaceholder can be seen through my roles as both a wedding officiant and spiritual counselor/life coach. When I officiate weddings, I hold the sacred space of that specific and important moment in time for everyone that is present (i.e. ritual facilitation). In my counseling and coaching practice, I hold the energetic container for the client to find their own answers as they express the feelings they need to work through. In my style, I also use my intuition to ask specific questions and observe the client's choice of words, energy, and body language to determine areas that are asking to be touched upon and investigated further. I'm also preparing to hold space when I *read the room* as I speak to a group of people, as well as when I prepare my mind and environment to write, and then as I allow the perfect words to find their way through me and into my pen or on the computer.

Holding energetic space and doing it well is a practiced art and requires energy, focus, and concentration. In recent centuries, our society has largely taught us that we have to be *doing* certain things in order to be of value, but the *being* of spaceholding is just as necessary for our balance and well-being. Also, because it takes so much energy, it can also drain us even more than the things that we may *do* in life.

Spaceholding is a feminine energy. Feminine energy in spaceholding involves creating a *container of allowing,* and then holding safe whatever wishes to be born within that space. Using the feminine energy of spaceholding runs contrary to the current inclination Western culture has toward focusing our energy on problems and then immediately jumping in with solutions that are created with the same mindset that created the problems. It is for this reason that the key words in the definition I provided of spaceholding are: *allowing* and *organic.* To create an energetic container, you must wait on the masculine energies of solving and doing as you put yourself aside and allow something higher and greater than you to come in and guide you or the person you are holding space for, toward the action steps needed to bring the highest and best outcome for everyone involved.

Just like baking a loaf of bread or having a baby, we prepare the environment and then allow things the amount of time they need to fully form. We all want to give things the best chance that we can of working out, be they relationships, conversations, situations, new job arrangements or collaborations, or just sitting with our or another's feelings when they come up and waiting until we can better understand them. Spaceholding is so important because if we say or do things haphazardly, or we *react* rather than *respond* to people, situations, or emotions, we may be taking an already murky situation and making it murkier. Sometimes the only way to get off the hamster wheel of repeating unhealthy cycles is to get ourselves out of the line of fire and remain an observer. This means not even stepping a foot into the situation until we are acting from a place of peace and wisdom. This is not to be confused with a *place of knowing*. We may think we know the answer or how we'd like to react, but it is actual wisdom—the kind that is present when our actions don't feel hurried, pressured, or taken on the spur of the moment. We all like to feel good. We like situations to feel good. We can end up causing ourselves even more issues when our undesirable or uncomfortable feelings come up when we try to rush in right away to *fix* them. Due to the fact that we are pleasure-seeking beings, if we are not fully conscious, we often immediately react to uncomfortable feelings by wanting to rid ourselves of them as quickly as possible. We try to push them down, drown them in other substances, project them onto other people, or to come up with immediate solutions to 'solve' our pesky issues.

Sometimes, all that is needed is for us to just hold space for those uncomfortable feelings and simply allow them to be there. Just *being* with ourselves or another, and often times not even saying a word, can be enough to allow the answers to present themselves. When we can do that, we find that many times their intensity will dissipate and organic solutions begin to show themselves. If the answers don't show up, at the very least, we are provided with enough breathing room in the situation to shift into a healthier, clearer energy before moving forward and attempting to *do* anything.

In holding this space, we have also not attempted to talk ourselves or others out of our undesirable feelings. Since all of our feelings need validation and observation in order for us to be truly healthy and not split things off into our shadow side (more on this later), this is a tremendously helpful tool.

Before I go much further, I would like to stop for a moment to ask, now that you have a better idea of what a spaceholder is, are you finding yourself able to immediately honor yourself for it and realize that it takes a lot of energy? Do you feel your self-worth growing as you look at your life and realize, "Yes, I am very helpful to myself and others when I step into the feminine energy of *being* and use my spaceholding talents." Another part of my motivation for writing this book is to make sure that you do. Even though it may not seem like you are actively *doing* anything and that this *being* shouldn't be taking up any energy, it most certainly does. Learning and perfecting the art of spaceholding and then honoring and exploring its value in your personal life will bring increased wealth, joy, understanding, and abundance to you and those around you. When your own life and those around you are affected, the outer world will undoubtedly be affected as well. If all of this can happen simply by you honoring yourself for further understanding something you are already doing, then you may just be one more drop in the pond of creating the peace and harmony so many of us seek in this world.

Preface-Definition of Terms

A Brief Overview of Masculine and Feminine Energies in Spaceholding

All humans and all creations contain both masculine and feminine energies. Feminine energies include timing, gestation, right relations, cooperation, thoughts, feelings, and the abstract. We are tapping into feminine energies every time we relate to a client or a friend, or when we enter the creative realm to write a book, paint a picture, or choreograph a dance. Masculine energies include order, logic, reason, and detail. They invoke such things as structure, the laying of plans, and the physical manifestation of ideas. They are the action steps that you take when the timing is right, and an idea is ready to move on to the next step.

Ideas are born in the feminine energy of the universal creative field. Masculine energies then provide the logic, reason, and material substances needed to bring those ideas into physical being. *Spaceholding* is where these ideas and relationships are gestated, born, and nurtured. As one holds space for themselves, another person, an idea, relationship, or event, the manifested outcome is being held in a sacred moment in time, until such time as the best outcome is able to be brought forth. When the feminine art of spaceholding is entered before any masculine action is taken, projects, relationships, and situations can be entered into consciously and with presence, providing a space for the highest outcome possible.

In order for balance and harmony to come to our world, the natural rhythms of yin and yang, and masculine and feminine must be allowed to exist and create with each other, instead of competing against each other. In order to get there, we need to go back and reclaim the feminine, and a large part of that is the art of holding space.

A Brief Overview of Self-Awareness Concepts Covered in This Book

Your *ego-self* is the part of you that is interested in self-preservation and how you present yourself to the world. It is the part of you that learns how to most successfully navigate your environment from the time that you are young. Your ego-self also helps you to manage all of the ways that you use to navigate the world in your earthly body, as well as decides the acceptability of the expressions and personality traits that you allow yourself to display. If you experienced trauma or undesirable experiences at an earlier stage in your life, your ego-self will do its best to protect you from ever repeating the same situation. The urgings of your ego self may or may not actually be in your best interest, depending on whether or not something that was a previous threat is applicable in your current life. Certain circumstances may have changed (i.e. being a helpless child at the time of the trauma) that might make the fear unjustified in the current stage of your life where you do have more choice and control.

The *shadow* side of you is made up of anything that you refuse to recognize in yourself. Shadow traits can include things that your parents or other authority figures told you were not acceptable about yourself, things that you saw others doing in excess or in an extreme way, behaviors or personality traits that you promised yourself you would never do or would never become, things you hold heavy judgment on others for, or things that you judge yourself for feeling no matter what the reason. Shadow traits can be positive or negative as anything we've disowned in ourselves for any reason becomes part of our shadow side. You may have some wonderful traits about yourself that would be very positive if allowed to express themselves fully through you, which are also hiding away in your shadow side.

Triggers are words, situations, gestures, etc., that when experienced spark an emotional charge in the person experiencing them. The emotional charge of a trigger most often points to a previous trauma or emotional wound that is still unhealed. The situation, experience, tone of voice, etc., feels to the receiver like a re-opening of these wounds though the present situation may be completely benign.

Mirroring is the spiritual principle that people and situations around you reflect back to your current stage of spiritual and personal growth. In many spiritual traditions, contemporary and ancient, the unwanted actions and behaviors of those closest to you, as well as any other obstacles you encounter in your physical life, are seen as opportunities for you to decide how you will respond to each situation or person in order to further your own soul growth. As a mirror, someone's behavior may help you uncover a part of yourself that either acts the same way or has the potential to act in the same way when you use your reaction to their behavior as a self-reflection tool. Mirrors can be tricky because the details of the circumstances can vary. Even if you think the other person's behavior does not at all apply to you, it is possible you may be acting out the same core trait in some area of your life. It takes thoughtful reflection and a willingness to look deeper to see where the similarity may be on a core level. Again, the reflections of yourself that you find in others who are mirrors can be both positive and negative.

A Brief Overview of Empaths and People With Energetic Sensitivities

A person who is energetically and emotionally sensitive to the feelings of others and energy around them is called an empath. An empath can pick up on another person's pain, fear, joy, elation, sadness, etc., without the person even needing to speak. Sometimes an empath can pick up the energy of what happened previously in a certain place, or even pick up on the emotions and feelings of a person who is not geographically anywhere near the empath. Empaths make extremely good confidants and counselors as they are able to empathize and feel the other person's emotions. *Empathic* and *energetically sensitive* are used in connection with describing an empath.

Similar to empaths are emotional or energetic sponges. In fact, many empaths qualify as both. Emotional or energetic sponges are people who literally cannot help but to soak up all of the feelings, emotions, and energies of everyone around them. Most empaths start out as emotional or energetic sponges until they become conscious of their tendency and learn how to separate their energy from that of others. Energetically sensitive people hold a very special gift, but life can also be somewhat difficult for them until they learn to work with and harness that gift in a healthy manner.

Specific Spaceholding Terms

An *energetic container* is a term directly related to the art of spaceholding. An energetic container is a space that is intentionally created by a spaceholder in order to safely hold any emerging ideas, emotions, feelings, or triggers, for the purposes of either healing or creating new concepts or things. An energetic container is formed when a skilled spaceholder focuses their energy (either consciously or unconsciously) toward maintaining an appropriate energetic space for the thoughts, needs, emotions, and actions of the present moment to emerge in a safe and allowing space.

Keeping things on track is something a spaceholder does within the energetic container that they are holding in order to energetically guide a person, group of people, or situation towards the highest outcome that can be born within the space being held.

Shifting is the process of changing a person's emotional state. Shifting occurs when a person's mood changes dramatically from what it was, or when the energetic space that was being held for a particular matter, mood, or emotion has been noticeably dropped, changed, or withdrawn. A spaceholder may need to shift themselves from their outside duties in order to be ready to hold space, and may need to help others shift either before, during, or after a time in which concentrated space has been held, such as in a meeting, emotional talk, or decision-making session.

The term spaceholder will be defined in detail throughout this book, as the definition and understanding of what a spaceholder is, and consequently, the honoring of oneself or others for providing this service are my major motivations for writing this book.

Spiritual Laws Covered In This Book

The *Law of Attraction* is a spiritual law that explains how the energy you are radiating (consciously or unconsciously) brings you similar experiences. Like attracts like, you get what you put your energy and focus on, whether wanted or unwanted and what you desire, desires you, are some examples of this law. Since the Law of Attraction also states that even your unconscious energy can attract things in similar energetic frequency, it is advised that you become conscious of your inner landscape when attempting to change what you are attracting to yourself if you desire something different.

A Personal Journey Through the Life of a Spaceholder

The Beginning of the Journey to Greater Self-Awareness

At some point in your adult life, the methods you used to employ in order to cope with childhood and early adult concerns are not as effective as they once were. You begin to feel as if you're not getting ahead the way you used to. None of it makes any sense as the same types of situations keep presenting themselves, and you are responding to them in the same way that used to work for you. At this point, it feels not only like things are not working the same, but now there is a mountain of uncomfortable feelings that are beginning to well up inside your heart. You are just not sure what you want anymore and have no idea why your old responses aren't working. At some point, after questioning, struggling, and becoming exhausted, you may finally decide to look at those feelings and investigate the sharp turn your life is taking. You are about to learn about holding space.

And thus begins your journey …

Allowing Yourself to Be Uncomfortable

As you surrender and begin to explore, the first thing you find is that there are many rich things to be explored in the depths of sitting with your feelings as they arise. Not needing to *do* anything about them, but to just allow yourself to feel them rather than shoving them away, pushing them down, or directing them misguidedly at other people. Taking responsibility for owning and working with (or even just allowing) your feelings is of prime importance if you want your relationship with both yourself and others to be healthier, happier, and more abundant.

Buried or medicated feelings do not just go away, they will continue to manifest in all different ways until you finally take a look at what you buried underneath the symptoms long ago. What you may have done as a child to cope with surroundings you could not control is no longer useful in your adult life where you *are* in charge. Working with and honoring all of your feelings in a healthy manner as an adult brings you into a conscious relationship with your life and helps you to respond in a manner of your choosing rather than allowing twisted versions of your buried emotions to run the show for you.

The most damaging thing you can do in relationships (and every aspect of life is built upon some type of relationship), is to take your uncomfortable feelings out on someone else, or to *pass the poison*. Not holding space for your feelings denies you the opportunity to see what those feelings have to teach or show you. Furthermore, flinging them haphazardly at someone else only magnifies the issue for them, yourself, and also humanity as the infection spreads.

What you now discover is that the first step towards becoming a master spaceholder is to learn how to hold space for *yourself*. You now take a step back and observe the events of your life and work with the feelings that come up and the reactions to them. You create an energetic container for yourself to work things out in learning the subtle art of holding space.

What are some ways to hold space for these uncomfortable feelings in yourself?

BECOME AN OBSERVER

The minute you feel the uncomfortable feelings, attempt to remove yourself from the situation. If you are not able to do this physically, you can become a mental observer. Imagine yourself not in the middle of the situation, but looking on at a distance. What do you see now? How do things appear differently? Resist the desire to respond or react at this stage for you will most likely do so from old patterns or coping mechanisms. Just take a step back and simply observe.

BREATHING/CENTERING

"Breathing through it" will help to take the edge off. Any kind of breathing practice you can start and maintain on a regular basis will be of tremendous benefit to you in developing this skill. If you can learn slow and steady breathing and centering (or any form of meditation) while you are calm and comfortable, it will be much easier to access this skill when you are uncomfortable. "An ounce of prevention is worth a pound of cure."

FEAR SITTING

Fear sitting is sitting in a chair for two minutes and allowing your feelings to have their way with you in a safe setting. They only get *two minutes*. Those two minutes may seem like two years, but if you can make it through the fear and perceived torture that you are allowing yourself to go through, you will find that you feel much more relaxed after those two minutes.

WRITING

Writing out your true feelings in a stream of consciousness fashion is a great way to bring down the level of uncomfortableness while feelings are raging in your body, begging you to look at them. Just take out a piece of paper and a pen or get to your computer and start letting it all out. Don't edit yourself, just let your words flow completely uncensored and see what you find.

TALK TO YOUR HIGHER POWER

Have a conversation in your head, on paper, or any other way you've found it to work for you, and ask your higher power why you are having these feelings. Let the first answer(s) come to you. You may be surprised at what you hear. In this case, it is also advised to develop a working relationship with this higher power and not go there only when you are stressed or in crisis (more on this in the next sections). If you find you are afraid or perhaps skeptical, consider that perhaps your higher power is not really as scary as it has been made out to be by either you or those around you. A relationship with your higher power is really no more frightening than a relationship with another person in the physical world. Use whatever reference works for you: higher self, God, the Universe, guardian angel, Spirit, perhaps even a loved one that has passed on.

TALK TO YOUR BODY/SELF/SOUL

Have a conversation with yourself. Ask why you are having these feelings and what action steps you do or do not need to take to bring down their intensity. You can do this through talking to yourself in your head, out loud, writing, muscle testing, or any other method that works for you.

WORK WITH A COUNSELOR OR LIFE COACH

The more you get your feelings out, the less they will need to overwhelm you to get your attention. Know that you may or may not need to *do* anything to help yourself process those feelings. They may just need to be acknowledged. A talented counselor or life coach should be able to pick up on the nuances of your statements or responses as you speak and be able to show you where the gold lies in your issues or problems.

GET SOME ENERGY OR BODY WORK

A massage or session with an energy healer can help to release the places where unhealed and buried feelings may have manifested themselves as physical knots in your body. A qualified and skilled body worker or energy healer has the ability to find these trouble spots and to break up the energetic knots without you even having to do anything!

When you realize that your old *responses* to familiar situations are not as effective anymore, you will come to realize that they were old coping mechanisms and were actually *reactions* rather than conscious responses. As you begin your new journey and become more self-aware, you will realize that sometimes you need the mind to come in and analyze, sometimes you need to take action steps, but sometimes all you need to do is to begin to bring these feelings out of the shadows and into the light. The hurts and injustices they represent will start to heal by themselves. The point is, you can create happier, deeper, and more joyful relationships with both yourself and others by taking personal responsibility for your own intense feelings when they surface, or by asking others if they can hold space for you while you take a time-out to figure things out.

Spiritual Connections/Consideratic
Holding Space

As you continue on your journey of discovery, you suddenly begin to understand that you can't figure this out all by yourself. There are greater concepts at work here, and the tools your physical caretakers and authority figures have given you along the way to use may have taken you as far as they can. You find that it's time to explore something deeper.

The Role of Intuition in Spaceholding

What role does intuition play in spaceholding? Developing a good relationship with and understanding of your intuition and higher power will help you immensely in spaceholding. Having a solid relationship with that which is greater than you (however you define or see that) will give you all kinds of advantages in knowing when, why (though you may not always know why right away), and how to do things. Listening to your gut instincts, in tandem with having a working relationship with your higher power, can make spaceholding much easier. You can even be guided on learning how to hold space.

Developing a consistent relationship with your higher power and learning to decipher your intuition may well be the most important tools and skills that you will ever develop in your life. Things start off as concepts or ideas first, and then the mind goes to work to figure out how to put them into action. Therefore, figuring out how to best work with the universal field that holds the space for all of creation will bring you to manifestation faster.

Taking things as they come, going with the flow, and living life minute by minute, will greatly help you tap into your intuition. However, we can only tune into those *gut* feelings when we are quiet and calm enough to hear and feel them. A good stillness or meditation practice will help you to slow down enough to hear the subtle voice of your intuition and/or higher power. Having a greater plan and goals ır life are a great start, but remember to also keep yourself flexible and fluid, allowing for shifts and changes along the way. If you get too caught up in the masculine energy of moving forward, action, and manifestation, you will drown out your inner voice. Like everything, balance is key. Living with your feminine and masculine energies together, and in partnership, will get you further and provide the most sustainable results for your dreams to become physical realities. Again, this is where dreaming, creating, and gestating in the feminine, and then going forward in the masculine, and then going back and forth as needed, are some of the most important life skills one can develop. This is similar to general shifting back and forth from the spiritual to the physical, in order to live a holistic life as a human on earth.

Intuition is also being used when we wait to be in the *right* space to do something. In order to have the best possible experience, it may be wise to hold off on doing something until we are in the right space for it. Timing is everything, as they say, and in spaceholding, this is absolutely true. Heeding your intuition, gut feelings, and working with your spiritual team works well here. Logic may tell you that it makes *sense* to do something at a certain time, or in a certain way, but your body and energy may have different feelings about it. In this case, it's best to stop and try to get a read on what is coming up for you. Is it just fear, and you just need to acknowledge it and is best to walk through it? Or is what you're feeling originating from somewhere else, telling you something you may not necessarily understand or even make any sense of, that seems to be asking you to wait for another time?

When you are developing your intuition, you might be working with things like symbols, colors, gut feelings, sounds, numbers, synchronicities, etc. There are many methods to use in getting your messages and having conversations including, but not limited to, automatic writing, talking to your celestial team either silently or out loud, asking for signs, or praying. When communicating with your higher power and ethereal team, just be careful that you are always in *partnership* with them and that you know you are talking to the most benevolent beings, not imposters pretending to have your best interests in mind. I find if I ask for certain beings they will answer me. If I get the slightest idea that something is off with their messages, I will ask up to three times if I am really speaking to the being that I asked for. The imposters can't handle that and you will usually know immediately if you are not dealing with the highest benevolent beings that you requested by name.

When using your intuition, conversing with your higher power, and receiving messages, know that your messages can be literal or metaphorical. Because you and your helpers are a team, you would be wise to always test things against your own heart and gut before you act on them without question. You may find you need to ask for more clarification, remind them about certain earthly concerns, or sit with things a bit more before you act. Developing your intuition and a relationship to your higher power is a very different process for everyone, and it changes all of the time. It takes time and practice and doing so is like fine tuning a radio dial when you are out in the country. Sometimes you get the station loud and clear, sometimes it is fuzzy, and sometimes it goes out completely. This is why I recommend developing a *relationship* and partnership with your higher power, rather than a blind following. You were given free will for a reason. It is your free will to establish this partnership, and it is also your free will to decide how you use it or flow with it. In the end, life is always about choices, and you are the only one who can make them for yourself. Working with your higher power and ethereal team is a way of partnering with the most masterful team of advisors in your life that you could possibly hope for, but you are still responsible for making the final decisions.

How Your Higher Power and Ethereal Team Hold Space for You

The supreme masters of spaceholding are God, or any preferred title for your higher power, and your benevolent team of angelic helpers and benevolent masters. These beings truly understand how to hold space for you. They know that though they are there to help and will assist you if asked, it would not be helpful of them to interfere with experiences that are for your growth and highest good. That is, they will not *over-help*. When they see you struggling, they are able to do what they can to assist you and help you to see what you need to look at, understand, or master, but they will not just rush in to save you if there is a higher purpose for what you are experiencing. They love you and watch over you and hold the strongest energetic container anyone can hold for you. Your surrender to a life in *partnership* with them, rather than forcing things to your own will, will almost certainly bring the results you are seeking. They may not be the results you thought you wanted, but your means of getting there will often flow more effortlessly if you work with your benevolent helpers and/or the flow of life, rather than against them.

Just like when space is held for a discussion between two people or a group, sometimes if you just get out of the way of trying to force or pre-empt a solution, one will very likely emerge out of the space held. In this case, if you have asked for help or handed your issues over to your higher team, you must then get out of the way and let them help you. All you really need to do is to just keep showing up and continuing to hold the space for yourself and to explore any fears or blocks that may be showing themselves to you, all the while paying attention to any directions you may get from them on any action steps you may need to take.

Your higher power and benevolent helpers are always holding space for you as you go along through life and work through things. They are always holding your highest good in mind if you'll just surrender to being in partnership with them (just as in any good and healthy relationship) rather than to exert your own will or armor or defend yourself against their contributions or assistance. If you let them hold the space for you, you will find it much easier to hold the space for yourself and others as you will be more balanced.

Asking and allowing them to help you does require a certain level of surrender, however, and, based on childhood experiences, the amount of this that you think that you can bear is different for everyone. Any trust issues or trauma with your very human childhood caretakers may need to be worked with and understood before you may be willing to consider a self-chosen surrender to a partnership with your higher power. If you unconsciously think of your ethereal parents and your earthly parents as the same thing, you may find that the idea of surrender, even to a partnership with them, will bring up some of your old authority issues. That is until you come to realize the very real difference between the two.

Also, remember that when working with your divine team free will requires that you must *ask* for help. Because they are such master spaceholders, they will lovingly embrace and guide you, but because of spiritual laws, they cannot jump in to help you unless you ask for help. Although you are here to learn and they will not take that away from you, I don't believe we are here to suffer unnecessarily, and it is always worth it to ask to see if they are able to be clearer with their guidance, or if they are able to bring out their protection and authority to change anything if you are really in over your head.

Personal Growth and Self-Care

At this point in your journey, you may have tried to hold space for others and perhaps given more than you could, or maybe you even tried to save or fix others. You may have drained yourself and started to question the validity of the old adage "do unto others as you would have them do unto you." It may seem that what it has really come to mean is that you are supposed to do so at the expense of yourself in the hope that others will then be able to hold you up. You may be starting to understand that there is more to it than that and perhaps there's a reason to secure your own oxygen mask first before assisting others. You are beginning to see that you cannot hold space for others until you learn how to put yourself and your needs first and then, and only then, will you be a full enough vessel to work on the skill of effectively holding space for others while keeping your own cup full.

Why You Should Always Take Care of Yourself First

It is a scientific fact that, if a pressurized cabin on an airplane loses pressure, you only have seconds to secure your oxygen mask before you pass out. For those of you who have ever been on an airplane, you've most surely heard, "Always secure your own oxygen mask first, before attempting to help those around you." The reason for this is that if the person next to you is a child, elderly, or otherwise disabled, and if they rely on you as a caretaker, what will they do without you if you secure their mask first and pass out?

I like to use this as a very strong metaphor for why it is imperative that people take care of themselves first, so they don't find that they are giving from an empty cup by trying to assist others in ways that they themselves are empty. It is also like trying to save a drowning person. Unless you have a good plan or are trained, there is a strong possibility that you will both need help if you jump in haphazardly, not fully able to take on the rescue that you are attempting.

In order to best uplift others, you will do best by uplifting yourself. We only have so much energy available to us at any given time. The stronger you are, the more energy you have to use on proper ways to inspire, teach, and heal others, without attempting to do their personal growth work for them.

Another reason it is best to take care of yourself as a holder of energy and space is that spaceholders are notorious for unconsciously transmuting the energy all around them all day long without even being aware that they are doing it. This is exhausting and draining, and you may sometimes need time alone or in your own space to recoup. Strengthening your own energy field by processing and transmuting your own triggers and issues consciously is important. Being unafraid to disappoint others, resisting doing things out of guilt, and making sure your boundaries are strong and firm, is another great way to take care of yourself and provide even greater service to those around you.

Please note that I am speaking mostly of personal growth and emotional situations, not those physical situations in which a doctor, ambulance, or other specialist is needed and should be called in order to offer physical/medical assistance and help when necessary.

In the case of holding space, you must be sure that you are filled enough and have ample energy available to assist someone else. If not, you should politely decline, or not answer the phone the next time a friend or family member makes yet another emotional *crisis call*. Instead, try resting in the knowledge that if your friend or family member really needs help or someone to talk to, that the universe will send someone else to fill that position. Again, this is a personal call based on you, your history with this person, and what your inner guidance, gut feeling, or higher power is suggesting for you to do in that particular case. Also, as in every case of spaceholding for others, be sure to check in with yourself to see if it is possible that you are attempting to rescue or fix someone, rather than just holding space. Either way, you and your spaceholding will not be much good to anyone if you are worn out. Even better, when you take care of yourself and your needs, you inspire others to do the same, rather than to give too much and then need to receive more than necessary from others. This helps to stop the nasty hamster wheel of people looking outside themselves for things that they should be able to provide for themselves through their higher power, intuition, and own inner resources and it strengthens everyone's energy as a result.

Taking Space for Yourself
Practical Tools for Taking Care of Yourself First

There are many times in life where it is beneficial for everyone involved if you know how to hold space for yourself. Today, this is still a very courageous thing to do as it is against the grain and involves a solid commitment to yourself that may rub others the wrong way. The benefit, however, is that when you take and hold space for yourself, new insights are allowed to emerge that you may not have seen amongst the noise and clamor of everyday life and relationships. When you are out there in the world and aren't in your little bubble, you are constantly taking in and attempting to transmute everything around you. Taking space for yourself to be still and just be in your own energy on a regular basis will help you to decipher what *stuff* is yours and what is others'. It will refresh and rejuvenate you after time spent in the energy of the world. Taking space for yourself involves unplugging from your usual activities in order to allow some empty space for healing, new insights, or just for energy rejuvenation. A regular spaceholding practice will usually involve some type of meditative activity, prayer, contemplation, or just stillness.

In addition to your regular spaceholding practice, you may find that you need extra space in order to work on a project, give more attention to someone or something, or to further your own personal growth of self-healing. Highly sensitive souls (which most evolved space holders tend to be) need to cleanse and recharge their energy tank often and may have already had to drop many of the unnecessary and over stimulating or energy draining activities or relationships in their lives in order to function at their highest. Sometimes, even those who are already cleared out and down to a pretty bare-bones external life, still experience moments when they may need to pull back their energy even further. They may need to more fully examine all that is in their lives and determine if further inner healing work or outer *healer* work in the world needs to be done. If you are feeling the pressure and a call to take a time out, your soul is telling you that something is out of alignment in

you need to step back and allow for some reflection
in order to get yourself back on your path. I have taken
extra space for myself in many ways over the years. I have
.idays, told people I was on retreat even though I was at
i.   d people I was being quiet, or that I was taking space for
myse. .o write. Knowing your energy limits and honoring your need
for whatever level of re-charge time is best for you is one of the best
things you can do for both yourself and those around you as a
spaceholder. It will help you to continue to be able to show up for all
involved in a much healthier manner.

Those people and activities that you may need to pull away from
may not initially understand your reasons and could very well feel hurt,
but for the sake of everyone's highest good, it is best to do what is
highest and best for you and not recoil out of guilt or shame. When we
are able to honor ourselves and our needs without shame or guilt, we
are better able to hold space for others and provide the same to them.
We also inspire them to allow themselves to do the same. By allowing
ourselves to have needs and to ask for them to be met, all of our needs
get met in a much healthier way and everyone is happier and freer. We
grow very strong when we can hold steady in ensuring this extra time
for ourselves. Not only do we grow stronger for what we may discover
during that quiet, open space, but we grow stronger for standing our
ground when we are faced with others who may not understand our
reasons.

Though the extra space you need may strain a relationship for a
certain time period, it can be minimized if it is done with kindness and
love and in a manner that uses *I* statements to explain why you are
taking the time and asking them to honor that for you. Those that can
allow you this time and still be there for you on the other side will either
have a closer, stronger relationship with you, or a more real one, even if
it changes or ends due to the things that you learned in the space you
took. In other words, those who are supposed to remain in your life and
are a benefit to you will still be there. If not, either they will leave, or
you probably have decided that your relationship with them is either
complete or no longer healthy for you and perhaps that's why you
pulled back in the first place. Either way, the authenticity now present

is surely of the utmost benefit to everyone involved, including the greater world, as you will now have more freed energy with which to share your gifts and talents.

You may find that you need to take this extra space for yourself with the same people over a period of many years, especially close friends and family. Again, anyone who is good for you will most likely still be there in some way and will enjoy a more honest and true relationship with you as a result. It is possible that after your absence they may not want to show up anymore or be there in the same way that they were before you pulled back. This is quite okay as well. There is obviously a reason why you took the space and time in the first place. If it is their turn to need to take space for themselves (even if they are doing it with a bit more anger, upset, or hurt than the neutral way you might have done it), then that is what is necessary for everyone's growth as well, and you should graciously allow them the same space they gave you. Even if they aren't using *I* statements or being as neutral or positive about it, the space that is created will still benefit everyone and is obviously still necessary, whether it is for healing, growing, learning, or letting go of old wounds.

Whether you are taking the extra space for a creative project, a retreat, your own introspection and healing, another relationship that needs more time and attention, or anything else you may need extra time for, you will have to learn the value of balance and the power of choice. We only have so much energy so you will benefit from having enough of a regular stillness and presence that you are able to make grounded and conscious decisions about what you *choose* to spend that energy on. Self-healing, projects, creations, relationships, etc. all take energy, and we just can't do it all. It is best at times, especially when you do take some space for yourself, to take inventory of your life, find out where your goals, dreams, and desires really are, and then find all of the places in life where you are currently expending energy and see if they are in line. Only each individual can choose what they most desire out of life and that will show up differently for everyone. In relationships, just because someone may not pick you to be in their life in a certain way does not mean that you are less than or unworthy, or even unloved, it just gives you the space and freedom to stop spending your energy in that way and to move along to other people whose goals, dreams, and energy do align with yours. You can also consider shifting the type of relationship that you and that person have, or that either of you is hoping to have, and adjust your energy expenditure to reflect that.

There is no right and wrong here, it is a matter of honoring ourselves and in turn honoring all those around us as we become more completely honest and authentic in who we really are and what we really have to give in every moment. When we hold the space for ourselves we can become more truly honest and authentic with ourselves and those around us. With those cards on the table and everyone's highest good in mind, your apparent *selfishness* can lead the way and everybody wins.

HOLIDAYS AND VACATIONS

Taking extra space for yourself by taking a holiday or vacation is indeed a nice getaway, but the energy of a vacation tends to be more about fun and play than about balancing and centering yourself. There is nothing wrong with that. Sometimes if you've been working too hard on self-growth and stillness, it may also be exactly what you need in that extra space. If that is not what you need, however, but you would still like a getaway, you can look for a vacation that will double as extra stillness or meditative time by looking into retreats or perhaps a sabbatical. These are best used as extras, in addition to your regular spaceholding practice, because in general you will want to make sure you are taking space for yourself on a daily basis and not just when you are able to get away for a while. In essence, you want to make a life for yourself that you will not *need* to get away from.

Honoring Yourself as a Master Holder of Space

If you're like me and have found that one of your major jobs on this earth is to be a spaceholder, the first and foremost thing that I would like for you to do is to **honor yourself** for this role

Because our society puts too little emphasis and honor on anything *feminine* and has pushed to the extreme the glorification of the masculine energies of do, do, do, and busy, busy, busy, there aren't many places in our society where *being* is an honored part of life. We are always encouraged to do something or to hurry up so we can do something else. Sitting in silence, playing, meditating, or daydreaming have been mostly reserved for children and yogis, and even the children have been talked out of it. The good news is that all of this is starting to change. The hard news is that you are on the cutting edge crew, blazing the new trail. You very well may be criticized; people who only know the *normal* way will not understand what you are doing. However, if you delve into cultures that don't degrade the feminine, you will see that the feminine energies of spaceholding by medicine people, in rituals, rites of passage, and all matters of community and familial relations have always been as honored and revered as the masculine.

Just because our culture does not yet fully understand the importance of your being and holding energetic space for humanity, this does not mean that you are not doing or contributing anything, or that you are being irresponsible. I remember once when I was deep into a few months of silence and stillness in my spiritual practice, someone came to my house, saw me in my lounge clothes and said, "What are you doing, sitting around the house eating bonbons all day?" To which I thought to myself, "You have no idea what I'm doing or how much focus and practice it takes to sit here in stillness and silence for hours on end." That silence, at the time, was completely foreign to me and a whole lot harder than most of the *doing* I had ever done. I continued to think to myself, "And by the way, if I were sitting here eating bonbons all day, so what!" I had done a lot of hard work on myself and not for a minute did I waver or go back to old ideas in thinking that I wasn't doing enough, that I was being irresponsible, or that I was a failure. I had a purpose, I knew what it was, and I was dedicated and focused on what I needed to do to achieve it, which ironically in that moment was not to *do*, but to *be*.

As I look back, I realize that what I was being guided by my higher team to do was to completely rebuild my life on a more solid, conscious, and spiritual foundation, and the long hours of stillness were my detox. This new foundation would allow me to step into my calling, something greater than I could even imagine at that time, but I trusted in the steps to bring it forth in me. Now don't get me wrong, I wasn't sitting in silence for twenty-four hours a day and shirking the responsibilities that I knew I had, but I also wasn't making up new ones that I didn't have just to feel like I was busy. And furthermore, as far as the lounge clothes go, if you're going to be spending a lot of time *being*, it's best to be comfortable!

As you learn to hold space and begin to understand and honor yourself, eventually you will discover that it is of no use, and is actually destructive, for you to beat yourself up for not doing things you feel, or your ego-self is telling you, that you *should* be doing. In learning to hold space, you will realize that there is a reason and timing for everything, and you will no longer hold yourself back with the shackles of shame, blame, or shoulds used only to punish yourself for absolutely no wrongdoing on your part.

How often have you had a gut feeling about the timing being off for something, but logic tells you otherwise? Perhaps there were other voices in your head as well, telling you to, "Get with it" or to, "Stop being lazy and get to work." These are out of balance masculine ideas. They are useful when used in harmony with the feminine ideas of gestating and creating, but very out of balance if they stand alone. Since everything has its season and one experience always builds upon another, there is always a time for everything. Through holding space, you will begin to honor yourself and your intuition and start to let go of letting yourself or anyone else guilt you for things that you have not been guided to, or felt the space was not open for yet, or things that you are doing that they don't approve of. Just by letting yourself off the hook and honoring yourself for knowing what you really should be doing, you will give yourself the space to breathe new life into things and situations, and this allows movement to flow again. Projects unfinished will begin to either take shape or fall away. If they take shape, you'll realize it's because the timing is now right, or they needed a new or different energy. If they fall away, you can begin to honor them for the knowledge, wisdom, and experience they have brought you, rather than dishonoring and blaming them and yourself for not finishing them or for their *not working out*. There are infinite possibilities for the amount of things we can create on this earth. We obviously do not each have the energy to fully carry out every idea that comes into our heads. Sometimes your thoughts or ideas are merely stepping stones to something else, and by holding the space for their proper gestation, you can begin to allow what is truly best for you to shine through. You can begin to lessen the pressure to finish or hold on to everything you start, and instead can begin to use your energy on those things that feel more aligned, whether due to timing or just a better fit.

This is a whole new way of looking at the process of how you create. Again, everything about creating goes back to the idea that new creations are seeded, nurtured, and gestated in the feminine energetic container, and then given over to the masculine energy for the action steps necessary to bring them into the world. If you look at it this way, there is no reason to judge yourself for the timeline you think your projects and creations should be on. For as I stated before in the examples of the bread and the baby, things are ready when they're ready, and no amount of forcing them is going to allow them to turn out the way we really want them to. If we love our creations enough, we will hold space for ourselves and for them, and we will honor our intuition and inner knowing, and just breathe through any rough spots until we get a course correct and are flowing again.

This way of honoring ourselves for being spaceholders also applies to relationships. If we can all learn to hold space and how to honor ourselves for it, we will begin to start honoring all of our relationships, and all of the seasons they go through. We will no longer judge ourselves or the other person for who was right and who was wrong if a relationship ends or we part ways. We will understand the purpose and beauty of the relationship, however long it may last, and whether it was mainly pleasant, or mainly challenging. We will stop beating up ourselves and others for the way things should have been or who was at fault, and realize that we may know the reasons now, later, or never, but that every relationship has enhanced our life in some way, even if it's only for us to know that we'd never like to repeat one like it. Once more of us learn the value of spaceholding, we will no longer blame ourselves for decisions we need to make to honor ourselves and others, for the highest good of everyone, even if those decisions are difficult, or cause a shift or change in our relationships.

Consider all of the great philosophers, thinkers, artists, and inventors that our culture so revered after they died. I'm positive all of them heard from someone at one time or another in their lives that they had their head in the clouds or were being irresponsible. But without their passion and knowing of the truth of how important a contribution to society their being in that frame of mind was, we would be without many beautiful, useful, and wonderful things, and ideas that got brought into *doing* after they were imagined and allowed to take root in the space being held by someone's *being*. This may be in direct conflict with many things you have absorbed from society and authority figures as you have gone through life. You may have been taught that you must always be working on something, or that there is no place for dilly-dallying or daydreaming. In fact, there is a very important place for both in our world and our individual daily lives. If we do not take the time to contemplate, play, meditate, or daydream, we cannot continue to dream our dreams of anything. Nothing new would be developed, and everything would stay the same and very static. It will take the poets, artists, and visionaries of the world to break the mold and show that what they have to give is as important as current ideas of how to win at life in the Western world. Not only do we need people who play on each side of the spectrum, we also need to allow ourselves to do so as well. Too much or too little of anything leaves us unbalanced. Balance will always seek itself out some way, somehow, even if we turn a blind eye to it.

Know that the world is trying to get back to homeostasis, to balance, and to a center-point. To go back to the indigenous ways of honoring the feminine and going to those energies first, before bringing in the masculine, is the only way to right how far we've gotten out of balance.

This doesn't mean that you will forever be being or spaceholding in the feminine and never take it to the masculine. Sometimes, part of the purpose of your being and holding space is so that you can collect energy and information, and stay in that space until it is time to reach out and use what you've learned. Spaceholders that operate largely back and forth between both the masculine and the feminine are usually best served by at least some level of self-employment, or by becoming entrepreneurs of some kind. There are also those that stay largely in the feminine. Those spaceholders do a lot of cleansing, holding, and transmuting of energy for those around them, as well as society and the world in general. They are desperately needed in their roles at this time, to help put things in place for a new, harmonious, and peaceful world.

So if you are one of a small number who's job on earth is to be a spaceholder, honor yourself and know that your strong faith and knowledge of your worth and value in your role is of the utmost importance in society and that others will most likely thank you later. For right now, we need **you** to believe in and honor yourself for what you do and contribute, no matter what anyone else tells you, or what opposite energies you are up against.

You are a faith-holder, space-holder, and wisdom keeper. You have not chosen a wrong or irresponsible path. You have chosen a highly important, difficult path, full of integrity and merit, and humanity cannot truly move forward into balance, harmony, and peace without you. We are all needed. The time for the degradation of the feminine energies is over. We all need both sides in order to sustain ourselves and grow and create in peaceful harmony on this earth. All are pieces of the puzzle, and we cannot get to harmony unless all of the parts are joined together in harmony.

How to Use Your Gifts to Your Advantage
(If you tend to unconsciously transmute heavy or negative energy)

The ability to sense and work with energy is a tremendous gift, but it can also feel like a curse in the earlier stages of life. When you have the ability to sense and transmute or clean the energy around you, often times you use much of your energy without even knowing that you're doing it. In order to use your gift in a healthy manner, you will have to learn to separate yourself from the energy, client, person, or the world in general, and to become very conscious of when you are doing this unconscious energy transmuting. It is all too easy for an energetically sensitive person to pick up on the fear or turmoil of those around them and attempt to absorb and transmute that energy for them. This just leaves the sensitive person drained or maybe even in physical or emotional pain, and the other person unable to fully take responsibility for their own issues, as they don't even know they are there. An energetically sensitive person can also have a hard time distinguishing their emotions and energy from others as they tend to serve as energetic sponges, soaking up almost everything that's around them.

WHEN YOU ARE AT HOME, WORK, OR IN OTHER SMALL GROUP SETTINGS

If you are emotionally sensitive, learning to really step back, draw in your energy, and focus on yourself, while just holding a space of love for those around you who are in pain or turmoil, will assist in pointing the responsibility back to that person who needs to take it. It will also challenge you to further work with and hone your gift so that you can help others, but not hurt yourself in the process. You can do your work, but you can't do anyone else's. If you can step back and take care of yourself while just holding a space of love for the other, then both parties will have the opportunity to take personal responsibility for their *stuff* and to grow stronger because of it.

If you are an energetic sponge, you may take on and carry people's stuff and not even know you are doing it. This happens often when those very close to you are glossing over their issues and not dealing with them. When you know in your heart that it is their stuff, either tell them about it, or send it lovingly back to them, and then move on. Discerning what is yours and what is not can get difficult when you feel confused and off balance, and you don't seem to be tuning into your intuition and guidance. At those times, you may not even be able to recognize that it isn't you that is off balance, that it actually *is* the other person.

I am beginning to see correlations between when people aren't owning the issues or feelings they need to look at, and when they insist they are fine. For instance, a person may look at me as if I am being very cranky or irritable, while insisting that they are just fine, even if they were very stressed or had a very emotional time just before. If this happens for you, you may begin to wonder where all of their emotion went and why *you* suddenly feel uneasy. If it doesn't seem like they looked at or figured out what they were feeling or dealing with, chances are it isn't yours and you probably picked it up unconsciously. "Here, you hold this for me, and I'll hold this for you," are destructive games that will not particularly free either of you from an energetic prison.

I believe the trick to unraveling the mess is this: If you are a person who is not afraid to look at and own your issues and your mood just isn't making sense, consider that it is quite possible that you are carrying the buried feelings that the other person gave to you to hold, and also possible that neither of you is completely conscious that the transaction even took place. The other person might genuinely think that they are fine, and sincerely wonder what is wrong with *you* in that moment. In these cases, there is most likely something really triggering them and they just can't stand dealing with it. Projecting it onto you as if it is your issue may just be their way of getting it off of themselves so they can get some emotional relief. This can all get very tricky as it is hard to decipher clearly when you are unsure, especially when the other person can get insistent and defiant that it's not their stuff. However, if they are not willing to even consider owning it, and you seem to have no emotional charge around it, you can also consider that the issue is theirs and not yours.

Additionally, if you know that someone close to you is processing some things and they seem to be trying to get in your space or hug you a lot, you may feel somewhat repelled by their energy and not know why. It is possible in this case that they may be also unconsciously trying to pass their baggage on for you to hold.

Yet another way to recognize these types of unconscious energetic transactions is when you are clearly aware that there is an issue someone needs to deal with, but they appear to be turning to other things in order to cheer themselves up or snap themselves out of it. Some things to watch for in this case would be turning to the computer, going out too much, buying things, eating more than usual, working more than usual, taking a spontaneous trip, drinking, video games, or just about anything else that you may notice they are trying to use to feel better or lift their energy. They may also start to act out in strange ways, deflect the issues, or blame you for things. You may feel annoyed with them without being able to put your finger on a reason. You may also notice that after the energetic *handoff*, the other person might appear visibly refreshed and lighter since you have just processed all of their issues for them without any effort or personal responsibility necessary on their part. Again, they may look at you with an, "I'm fine, what is your problem?" attitude. They will expect you to shift to a different mood as fast as they have because now they actually *do* feel better. They will want you to feel better, too, as they no longer need you to carry the weight for them or to help them feel better by commiserating with them.

The best way to deal with situations like these is to continue to own your own power and worth and to find out where you are leaking energy and inadvertently taking on other's feelings and issues to process for them. You may also need to gently point out to them what has happened or just return their stuff to them for proper processing. Once you've untangled the mess and discovered what happened, be sure to also give yourself time to rest and recuperate. You'll have expended a lot of energy, both by carrying the other's stuff as well as by trying to understand what was going on with both your mood and theirs. Take some time for yourself to properly take in what you have learned about yourself and the other person, even if the other person feels better and desires to be in your space or in your energy.

The good news about all of this is that as you continue to practice this process, you'll begin to grow stronger, and the people in your life who will not or cannot seem to take responsibility for their issues will begin to either exit your life or start to transform. Know that continuing to take on other people's issues and being an emotional sponge once you become conscious of it would be an affront to both yourself and society since you would not be maximizing your gifts to their highest potential. Your emotional awareness and energy sensitiveness is a very positive gift once you really learn how to properly work with it. It doesn't do anyone any good if you process things for other people with the intentions of saving or rescuing them. Not only do they miss their opportunity to grow strong and empowered, but you weaken yourself as well. In order to really transform yourself and the world, you must allow yourself to rise up into your fully empowered self, and then inspire those around you to do the same. That way we all thrive.

WHEN YOU ARE AROUND LARGE GROUPS OF PEOPLE

As an emotionally sensitive person who is learning to use your gifts to your advantage, taking care of yourself may also include staying out of the line of fire. When the macrocosm of the world seems to be going a little wild, or drama seems more stirred up than usual, you may be guided to stay inside and keep to yourself, or go outside and commune with nature on your own or with a friend. Since you are always picking up and clearing the energy around you, those times when the world is going through major shifts may be times when you are best off staying in your own energy and not mingling it with those around you lest you get pulled off your center. During those chaotic times out in the world or in the cosmos, it is best to just keep yourself out of the line of fire, rest, and rejuvenate yourself, so that when things calm down you can emerge again.

Remember, one of the major duties of a spaceholder is to be a calm and wise presence when things get a little topsy-turvy. Know that the energy that affects others in big ways is also affecting you, and you have to work extra hard during those times to keep your balance. There is nothing wrong with resting and conserving your energy during these times as it is simply part of your job description for keeping yourself and those around you energetically healthy. Again, energy work might be of major help to energy sensitives who knowingly and unknowingly work with others and transmute energy all day. Replenishing your own tank and rebalancing where your energy has shifted can be of great help. In time, many empaths deal with the intense energy of the world at large by learning to be "in the world but not of it" as a means of keeping their energy separate from all the energy around them.

USING YOUR GIFTS TO YOUR ADVANTAGE

Please do not blame yourself if you discover that you are carrying or transmuting other people's issues, whether consciously or unconsciously. This is one of the hurdles you must cross when you have such a magnificent gift as emotional sensitivity. Only once you've truly mastered it will you be able to teach and show others how to work with and maximize their gifts. If you are still working with yours, know that you are still in a stage of apprenticeship with the universe and that you will be allowed to fly when you have truly mastered and embodied the power and wisdom that your gift contains. We are all students before we become masters of anything. Being unaware of the gifts and talents that we may be working on mastering should not be cause to shame ourselves, but only to understand that we may be dealing with something much deeper and more complex than we would ever have imagined and to know that we have a great responsibility to see it through.

Understanding and Directing Your Energy and Setting Energetic Boundaries

In relationships, especially if you are energetically sensitive, you may need to create boundaries, step back into your own energy for a bit, or say "no" to something without worrying whether or not you're the bad guy or girl. Holding space for yourself and others when you're an empath can be particularly challenging if you don't realize where you end and others begin. If many of the feelings you have actually belong to someone else, or you are attempting to hold, fix, or transmute their energetic issues for them, both of you can remain trapped in a never-ending cycle of recycled energy. You only have so much energy to give, and only you can know where you tend to leak it. If you automatically clean up other people's energy, you may need to do whatever is necessary to close off that faucet so you won't continue to leak your energy.

Much like our digestion and elimination systems, we must clean, cycle, and replenish our energy often. If we are continually giving the same energy back and forth to each other, we're holding ourselves and others captive, and neither of us will actually be able to take that next step forward into our greatness. Being tuned-in to our own energy accumulation and elimination system will help us tune-up our own bodies, minds, and spirits, and allow us more fresh energy to use towards the forward movement for ourselves and others. If we do not clean and replenish our energy, and instead just keep holding others' or giving them ours to hold, we remain stagnant and stuck in one place. Our energy is like a gas tank. If we are on empty, we have nothing left to give or expend for ourselves. If we are full, we have enough for ourselves and others. If we are somewhere in between, we need to be consciously aware of where that energy is going and be sure to balance what we are using with where we are refueling ourselves.

Remember to take care of yourself first, and know your limits. If you know a situation will be too much for you, have the courage to say no and explain how it will/is hurting you if the boundary you have to put in place affects someone else. If they are really meant to be in your life, they will do the best they can to respect and understand your limits and not to do anything that will harm you if they can at all avoid it.

Taking space and exerting our boundaries with those we love can be very upsetting at times. If things are swirling around, people are unaware of their issues, and the empath is unsure where his or her energies are leaking out, problems can result. If you are the empath and you attempt to heal and transmute any heavier energy your loved one may be carrying, it may be best for you to step back and create boundaries based on what is healthy for your energy and what is unhealthy. This would not be a good time for being timid about what you need in order to be healthy. You need to take care of yourself first because you won't be any good to anyone else if you aren't doing and feeling your best. Besides, if you are not transmuting their energy *for* them, they will eventually be forced to grow by having to deal with it themselves. This is a win-win for both parties.

Energy is an interesting thing. We all carry different levels of it at different times and we all spend it in different ways, both knowingly and unknowingly. When something feels uncomfortable just do yourself and those around you a favor and tell them that you are uncomfortable, that something is causing you hurt or pain or is draining your energy. Later, when you know why or what is causing your discomfort, you can begin to make empowered decisions about what you will participate in and what you will not. When you do not know why, it is best to stop and to *leave the conversation open* to be analyzed at a later time.

Explain to others in the best way you can how your energy works and how these things are hurting you. Those who are in a place to really love you will support you and want to find a way to work with you on this. A quick example of this is when people wanted me to watch loud, action packed movies that severely scrambled my energy. Once I realized I was *choosing* those movies for entertainment, I realized that I didn't need to intentionally cause myself to feel unbalanced and scattered. I just let people know which movies I could handle and which I couldn't and what they did to my energy, and that was that. Again, it was a win-win for everyone in that it helped the others since I certainly wasn't going to be any fun to hang out with if I was irritable and cranky after the movie.

In making sure that you are taking care of you first, you may also need to examine any self-worth issues that could be blocking your ability to do so. You may be fighting battles with old voices in your head, or maybe you don't think you even have the right to be free. You just need to take a look at where you are directing your energy and re-direct it towards what you really want to achieve. Don't let old voices in your head run the show. For example, if you rush to take care of others is it perhaps because somewhere along the way you were told or felt like you didn't have value just for being you? Did you decide somewhere along the line that in order to be worthy of love you had to become useful and *earn* your worth? If so, you may want to examine how and why you are allowing yourself to give whoever said or did that to you so much power. We are all worthy of love just for being ourselves. While you may not be a good match for one person, another might find your *being* to be of tremendous value. This is why your self-worth should not depend on anyone else. If you measure yourself by what others think, you may constantly get different opinions and never truly believe that you are worthy of being loved by another. In this way, creating boundaries is just a way of honoring your energy and making sure that you have plenty of gas not only to run on, but to thrive and create, making your cup so full that you have an overflow left to help others.

This may all seem very tricky, but with practice, you'll begin to own your value and be firmer in making sure your energetic needs are taken care of as a priority. It is more difficult to give others anything of rich value if your own energetic cup is not filled. Moreover, the more you take responsibility for your own energetic needs, the more you'll find that others begin to do so as well.

At some point, we won't need to hold as much space for ourselves, others, and our dreams—we'll be living them. It only requires one small, uncomfortable jump off the cliff of *same-old, same old*, to re-direct our energy and re-invent ourselves anew into the full glory of who we truly are.

The Spaceholder in Personal Relationships

You have now learned how to take care of you, as a spaceholder, and how to conserve and fill your energy reserves as well as how to honor yourself solely for your *being*. As the journey of your life continues, you will also need to understand more about how to navigate relationships with the gift you are learning to cultivate.

Why Others Might Resist You

Spaceholding is something that may not be understood by those around you. Those who are uninterested in personal growth or healing—who are caught up in the *hurry, hurry* lifestyle of our society, or the *problem-fix it* way of handling things—may intensely resist you and this way of handling things. Most likely these people have never heard of spaceholding. They may balk against, and even get angry at, the time it may take you to do things or to make decisions, or they may think that you aren't really *doing* anything, or think perhaps that you're not *working* hard enough at life. They may attempt to bully you or try to guide you towards a more *logical* approach. They may also be very resistant to why you do things the way you do.

Finding the courage to remain true to your known path and holding your center in the face of this resistance, is done by remembering this alternative perspective: True understanding of the value of spaceholding requires a shift from a mindset of *busy and productive* to one of *mindful and conscious*. The first *might* bring faster rewards, but sustainably, you will not usually get the results you wish for in the long run. Practicing the art of holding space can help situations, friendships, love relationships, crisis situations, grief, and all situations where we relate to others. Since all of life is interrelated, there is no place where perfecting the art of relationships would not benefit all of life on earth.

We can look at the fact that since we have been conditioned in Western culture to over-favor the masculine energy of action, those who unfortunately have not yet been supported in bringing in their feminine sides (due to cultural, familial, and gender conditioning) will most likely be resistant to your using of the feminine energy of holding space. They are not familiar with it and do not yet understand its importance. We all long for peace and harmony, but those of us in certain cultures were not raised to understand that we need both the feminine and the masculine energies to bring forth sustainable and lasting creations. In dealing with our feelings or life's challenges, the over-emphasis of the masculine has taught us to approach every issue by attempting to immediately jump in, fix it, or solve it.

In order to restore balance, we need to bring back the state of *allowing*—allowing seeds to be planted, the proper gestation of the ideas, and then nurturing them forth in their proper timing giving them the best chance of success and smooth sailing. Nature, as a whole, is designed to use the feminine energy first, and then bring the masculine energy in to carry forth the ideas that were created, gestated, and formed in the feminine container, but this has not been largely embraced by Western science. As *holding space* as a general term is a relatively new concept and not yet a meme, or practice that is fully integrated into society, it's going to take a few brave warriors, on the bigger stage and in our own homes, to lead the way until we achieve the "hundredth monkey effect" and more people gain a new understanding and jump on board. Healing ourselves and our split between the masculine and feminine will help to bring about the needed re-balancing of our world and begin to tip the scales back to neutral in many respects.

As a spaceholder, even though the greater populace is still highly unaware of the extreme value of holding space, you must know and fully believe in its value yourself and be willing and able to allow yourself to receive what you need from other places and in equal measure to the energy that you are expending in your spaceholding. If you find that you are not being balanced and you are growing weary, you may need to do less spaceholding for others and more for yourself until that energetic balance is more steadily in place and your needs and desires are being met more often. We are still going uphill for a bit, and you will need to stop and rest often to rejuvenate yourself until the masses understand spaceholding and are able to carry more of the weight.

Do what you can to hold your ground when you really believe in the space you are holding and remember to go to your higher power for help, support, and guidance. Also, know that although you may not be the most popular person in the room right now, those who initially resisted you will come back to thank you for your grace, poise, and strength when they realize the benefit it has had to them.

Spaceholding takes a tremendous amount of energy, so remember to take good care of your own energetic needs. This can be tricky, but I've found that as you get better at being stronger and more honoring of yourself and your own worth, you'll pick and choose where you do this for others. Eventually, their resistance will roll right off of your back. However, due to the fact that it does take a lot to hold that space when others show resistance, remember to honor yourself as to when and where it is most beneficial to use your energy in this manner.

Spaceholding to Protect Yourself and Your Relationships When Others are Out of Alignment, Unbalanced, or Angry

Space holding can also be used to protect yourself from getting sucked into other people's drama that has nothing to do with you. If you find yourself in the vicinity of a person who is unconscious of their issues, who is getting angry, spaceholding can help serve as a suit of armor to protect you from taking on or taking in anything that is not yours to absorb or work through.

People's issues and emotions are personal to them and can help them to see and understand areas of their lives that need to heal. When dealing with those that are not yet conscious of their triggers and the areas that need and desire their attention, spaceholding is a useful tool towards harnessing and creating a personal container for your own energetic field. Taking responsibility for our own emotions is one of the most important things each one of us can do to bring our planet into peace and harmony. The highest goal is for everyone to become conscious of their own *stuff* and then to use it for their own growth. Until that happens, spaceholding, or refusing to accept someone's projections or perhaps passive-aggressiveness, will be the best tool you have to deal with the emotions and triggers around you that have nothing to do with you.

Spaceholding around angry or triggered people keeps us from giving them what they want—a sparring partner to help them battle the wounds and uncomfortable feelings that they don't know how to deal with in a healthy way. This doesn't mean that we may not also need to respond, but it does mean that when we do respond, we will energetically decline their invitation to the fight, and therefore leave them with their true feelings and emotions to be brought up again and again until they begin to become conscious of them. It may take a great amount of energy to hold this space, but if we engage in their fight, both parties lose a substantial amount of energy. Nobody wins and the person will never see the issue that truly needs attention and the healing that only they can attend to.

Spaceholding can sometimes be seen when someone becomes very Zen like when others' emotions are swirling around them. Just like Switzerland, the spaceholder refuses to participate in the war and keeps their energy entirely to themselves. When a spaceholder can maintain their balance and avoid an energy leakage by not getting caught up in the chaotic emotions of others around them, their personal energy reserve becomes much stronger. Without directly doing anything specific, those around the spaceholder will be directed back to themselves and forced to either look at their emotions or to find someone else that is interested in playing this energy drain game at the expense of looking at their emotions.

If you can manage to avoid or to take some space from the person who is struggling or out of balance, many times that will be the easiest way to continue to hold space for the situation and the relationship. However, if you are in a situation where you will be seeing this person on a daily basis, pulling into yourself and concentrating only on your own things or setting appropriate boundaries with them will help you greatly with this conundrum. Again, doing whatever it is that keeps you balanced will make dealing with others much easier.

There are times when an understanding of whatever the person who is struggling is dealing with can actually be of benefit to those closest to them. If people are traveling through life as a unit, be it a partnership (romantic or otherwise), or a family (personal or business), sometimes the unit as a whole will not really be able to move forward in a healthy manner until the person struggling can uncover and become aware of their issues. At these times, it may be of benefit to the whole for the member who is best at spaceholding to encourage the other member to seek help, or at least not allow them to project their feelings onto the spaceholder or the others in the family or group.

Of course, if the person stays unconscious of their issues and is harming or greatly holding back the rest of the family unit, the other family members in charge may have to take some space for themselves to do some real soul searching on what is best for the health of the family. This, unfortunately, never seems to have an easy answer. Like anything, it is best when spaceholding and taking time out to observe and consider unhealthy patterns is done at the onset of a relationship in order to prevent issues later.

Interesting also to notice is the case of someone around us being passive-aggressive. In this scenario, a person will not desire to understand, nor be able to deal with their emotions, much less to process them. Many times their uncomfortable emotions are related to or can lead to anger. When someone is so out of touch with their emotions and only knows that they are uncomfortable, they may poke others by any means possible until the other person is as uncomfortable as they are, erupts, and then acts out their anger, despair, grief, or sadness for them. In this case, the spaceholder may need to nip this behavior, call it out, or reduce contact with the person until they are able to recognize and process their own emotions. An important thing to note is that you can be the best spaceholder in the world and still get sucked into a game of passive-aggressiveness if the other person is desperately uncomfortable enough to know just how to get you to act out their grief or anger for them.

Just to reiterate, the advice and comments in this section (as well as this book) are a general concept. Spaceholding in this way may not be sufficient enough in all situations, but is still a useful skill for everyone on the planet to learn. Until the masses can learn to become more conscious of, and to work with, their emotions, spaceholders will be needed to buffer and re-direct the misguided energy and unprocessed emotions that are spewed into the greater energetic field of the atmosphere every minute of every day.

I would like to stress here the importance of self-care, self-worth, and healthy selfishness for the spaceholder. Just as a teacher cannot be everyone's teacher, a computer programmer can't constantly be fixing their family's computers, and a therapist can't be counselor to their own family, the spaceholder needs to be sure that their needs are being taken care of, that their cup is full, and that they are maintaining appropriate boundaries with themselves and others. In addition to honoring themselves, they should also look to see if they are being balanced out and taken care of in other ways in order to recoup the energy they are giving out- just like if they were working at a job that paid in dollars.

As you read this section, know that I am not asking you to become a victim in any way. What I am suggesting that you do is to take an overall energetic inventory of your life and see if there is any chance you are cutting yourself short in your spaceholding duties. Consider the broader areas in which you may be receiving in equal measure to your giving, but the exchange might not be coming from the same sources that you are giving to. The world is intertwined and things are in play in many areas at the same time, all serving many of our purposes. It is possible that your needs and desires are being met in some other area of your life by some other person or source. It is also quite possible that your needs are being met and you just can't see from the world-view that you are holding how that is occurring.

Above all, remember that you deserve to receive, that you have needs, too, and you have every right to expect equal and reciprocal partnerships with others. Your spaceholding for others is a valuable service and takes up your valuable energy. If you are not being taken care of, it is probably the case that *you* are out of alignment and need to direct some of your spaceholding energy back towards yourself.

MIRRORING

When someone around you is not acting in their center or is pushing your buttons, there may be something to learn from why you are getting triggered in addition to needing to put up energetic boundaries between the two of you until they are able to take personal responsibility for themselves. It is a fine line to walk, but mirroring is when the person pushing your buttons is helping to show you something about yourself. For example, if they seem to be stopping you from getting ahead, maybe there is some unconscious part of you that is stopping yourself from getting ahead as well. In this instance, if you don't look at whether or not they are a mirror for you and believe that they are at fault or not in balance, you may be missing a major key toward better understanding yourself. Many times, when those around us are repeatedly acting out, there is something to be seen in ourselves from their behavior. Once you own this part of yourself and deal with it, many times the person's behavior will cease. However, there are also just as many times where it is completely the other person's issues and it may be necessary to create boundaries with them or reduce contact with them until they can own their part of the equation. Just be sure not to miss a chance to learn something from your messenger.

Holding Space in Relationships Until They "Come Around Again"

In our closer relationships, a time may come when people are not matching up enough energetically to facilitate a healthy relationship. The people may be on two different planes and the relationship may seem to be strained, dysfunctional, unhealthy, or just out of alignment. In these instances, if talking isn't working, it may be best to just give the relationship, or the person, some space.

There are times where it is better for both people to completely let go of the relationship and stop giving it any extra energy. If it's unhealthy and draining on either party it could be time to move on. In this case, these types of relationships may or may not eventually come around again, and one or both parties will need to do the emotional work necessary to truly let go of any attachment to a particular outcome.

In other instances, however, there could be something else at play. Perhaps one person needs to grow more in certain areas or heal an old wound that may or may not have anything to do with the other party. These are the types of relationships where the people involved know that they are never truly over and that some work and time will need to be given on either side. To try to force a solution could cause a backslide from the relational harmony being sought.

In these cases, it is best to go about your own business while placing that relationship to the side until it organically comes around again. This can best be used in life-long relationships that don't directly affect the course of your everyday life such as friendships, or relationships with family members or extended family. If this happens in a spousal or romantic partnership, sometimes it is best to just go about your business as you step out of the closeness of the relationship while still holding space for the highest outcome by extending your kindness and love during that time. This is not an easy task. However, the opportunity to explore the core foundations and connections of your love will most certainly be worth it as they bring forth greater sustainability, a more solid foundation, and ultimately, an even *greater* closeness.

Since a family relationship is one you can never truly completely let go of, if you need to establish boundaries or things are just not matching up energetically, holding space until the relationship comes around again will be a wise and helpful tactic to use. Some of our most challenging relationships occur within our families of origin, but most of us are not ready to completely cut the ties with these people. Most of us, even when we are struggling, secretly wish for forgiveness, healing, and a new beginning, so we may enjoy the depth that can occur from a new relationship with the same people we've formerly experienced conflict with. Ultimately, if we do choose to step away from family members for a while, we need to love ourselves enough to know that we are doing what we are doing out of love for everyone involved and that love isn't always about getting what we want, but more in doing what is right.

Tools for How to Cope When Someone "Needs Their Space"

How do you hold space for someone when they say, "I just need my space?" When someone tells you this, it can trigger old abandonment or rejection issues if you have any. In these cases, the very best thing you can do is to oblige and give them their space but do so in a way that you maintain the greater relationship you have with them. Let them know energetically, through word, action, or deed that you are still there and love them, but that you will honor their space until they have either shifted energetically or worked things out. Many times the person's need for space has nothing to do with you, but may be a need they have for silence or stillness in order to work something out so they can come back to you with a clearer mind, body, and spirit. If you take it personally, you may be holding back some very important work that can potentially improve the relationship that person has with themselves, as well as the one they have with you. If you can allow the person their space, many times they will be so relieved of the pressure, they might come back to you faster than you thought they would. On the other hand, if they don't come back at all, they have at least had time to be honest with themselves and you about what they're able to take on at that moment.

Similarly, you may also be the one to need space. Tell them that you want the space in order to best understand your potential triggers or just to feel refreshed enough in your own energy to be able to intertwine it with another's again. Maintaining and protecting our personal and energetic space is a very natural thing and is something all of us need to be healthy. If either of you is having trouble with it, try to estimate the amount of space that you might need and the approximate time it may take. Overestimate if you need to. This will give the other person more security around the fact that you will be back if you plan to be, and they then can get on with the things that are best for them until you return.

Although taking space for ourselves is a natural tendency, many of us still feel uncomfortable asking for it or allowing someone else to take it. We may be afraid that doing so will push the relationship further away, rather than bringing increased closeness and intimacy. The conundrum is that we need both independence and interdependence with others at any given time. Neither state of being exists without the other. Both are necessary to maintain balance and harmony, both in oneself and in one's relationships. Allowing ourselves and our partner to take the necessary space, while trusting that the relationship is still solid, permits more closeness and intimacy, even when it may seem like it would bring the exact opposite.

Though there is no magic formula for just how much space a person may need, it's a paradox that must be accepted and integrated into one's being, as every relationship will come up against it, even in one's inner relationship. Understanding and embracing this anomaly will ultimately lead to more freedom and satisfaction is your life and relationships. Again, we don't necessarily have to fix or understand the paradox, only to allow and accept it as one of life's mysteries, one of the universal laws of life.

Holding Space for Friends or Family Members
When They Need to Fall in Order to Get Back Up On Their Own

Almost all of us at one time or another will find ourselves in the role of supporting someone in need. It can be very tricky to balance when to offer or give physical help, and when to just hold space for them as they experience what they need to experience for their growth. Many of us have been taught the overly masculine way to save or fix people. However, many times the best thing we can do for others is to offer a listening ear and energetic support and love while also remembering not to take on more than can successfully be held. Knowing how to balance is the spaceholder's task.

Being a very tuned-in spaceholder myself, I have often liked to step in and offer assistance when I could see that it was needed. In fact, that's what my family taught me you *should* do. I used to burn myself out getting involved in trying to solve other peoples' problems. One day someone told me that it was quite possible, in many situations, that I was actually harming the very people I was trying so hard to help by taking away one of the opportunities that they had been given to work through their issues and grow stronger. In effect, I *wasn't* helping. I had never thought of it that way before, but to someone who was only expending all of that extra energy to help, finding out that I was actually possibly hurting those I was trying to help was enough to get me to take a good hard look at what I was doing. I realized that what I was doing was in direct correlation to the fact that it made me feel safer as a child to process people's emotions for them. I was shown that you must always help people when they were suffering and that to jump in immediately was the right thing to do. Holding others safe and allowing them to work it out on their own was not yet known or understood in my family. There was still leftover fear and processing of my grandparents' and their parents' feelings and emotions, and this perpetuated the family and societal meme. Therefore, as a budding spaceholder in my childhood, it felt much safer to me to process others' emotions so I could be safe because certainly I wouldn't be if I let them process and work things out on their own. If I did that they would never figure it out and come back to me, and then I would perish! And, if I could see their issues clearer than they could, well certainly it would be up to me to show them.

Once you work through some of your past issues, coping mechanisms, and fears, you can then add discernment to your spaceholding to help you determine whether someone needs actual assistance, or if they are best served simply by your presence. Using this discernment will allow you to more effectively help those that you are trying to assist. Our society may have us believing that a pint of ice cream and a shopping trip is the best way to care for a hurting friend. While that may be exactly what is called for, much of the time it is not actually helping. Holding the space for them is a way of empowering, rather than disempowering your friends and family, and a means to everyone's greater freedom. You do not want to train people to look to you as their savior, but to allow them the space to look to their higher power and within themselves first, before they look to friends and family for assistance. Please note, however, that even if you are a master spaceholder, it is not advisable for you to point out everyone's *stuff* for them if you haven't been asked to assist. And even if you have, be sure that you are either doing it in a professional setting or if in a personal setting, in a way where you are empowering rather than disempowering them, as well as allowing them to take their opportunities to strengthen themselves and find their own answers.

This is not to say that we will never need physical assistance from our earthly friends or that we might not need their assistance in emergency or crisis situations. However, when the opportunity dictates a time ripe for growing strength, faith, or a new understanding, we have to know when it's best to back off, and not to play God.

Holding Space for Yourself and Others in Order to Affect "Real Change"

Things will change on the outside when we truly transform on the inside. This is why rushing in to fix someone else's problems or issues never really works. It is imperative that the other person figures things out for themselves. Once they've hit the closed door enough times maybe they'll decide that they really want something different and truly believe they are worthy of receiving it. They will never be able to get up and truly stand on their own if they haven't gone through what they need to in order to cause a more lasting shift on the inside—the kind of shift that will allow them to continue to receive good things in their lives. Life gives us these *failures*, lessons, and fall-downs so that we can get over ourselves and any of the unconscious voices that we haven't freely chosen; that are still playing in our heads and making our choices for us. We will not be able to achieve our dreams if we don't believe we are worthy of them. Our problems and issues are often situations where we are being shown what we are not allowing to manifest in our lives. Then, we more successfully remove those blocks and allow ourselves this receiving.

The next time someone has a problem and you kick into high gear again trying to come up with solutions, remember that the time right when a problem occurs is ripe with opportunity for learning, observing, and releasing repeating patterns and letting go of old programming. It is a perfect time to release old programming and untruths that are telling them they aren't worthy of receiving joy, health, or abundance in some areas of their lives. Hold space for them during this time and love them through the uncomfortableness. Don't try to solve it. Love them, or ask them questions that lead them back to themselves or their own answers, but try not to offer solutions to their issues. This does not mean that you cannot help them solve the issue. However, the longer you can learn to hold the space for them, whether remotely, by their side, or by talking them through whatever feelings or triggers come up, the better chance they have of healing their issue and moving forward. In this way, you *have* helped them solve their issue by empowering them and allowing them to do it themselves, to grow stronger for it, just not in the way you may have thought.

We all get to decide the quality of life we live. No matter what the situation, there is always hope, and there is always faith, even when all else seems lost. If you work with the universal *Law of Attraction*, you can decide what you want rather than focusing on what you don't want or what you are afraid will happen. In this way, you'll be watering the garden of abundance rather than lack. In order to do this, you must uncover what it is that you are afraid of, and what voices, memes, or thoughts of limitation are telling you what is possible for you, that are unconsciously ruling your subconscious mind.

The best time to pull these things up is during the opportunities our souls give us when we are presented with obstacles, issues, or problems. At times, we are given these issues and problems in order to see our blocks. If we try to solve our pesky issues too quickly, we may miss the bigger gift that is hidden in the issue. We might have understood had we slowed down a bit, observed everything that was going on, and taken a breath or two, a gift that would help make a lasting change in perspective could be in the making.

So the next time you, a friend, or loved one has an issue, remember that it is also an opportunity to take a time-out from regular life, an opportunity to come from a different space, and see everything from a different angle, leading to a more sustainable and lasting change.

Being Honest With Yourself About When and How Much Space You Can Hold for a Partner

When you are in an equal and conscious partnership and you have the need for your partner to hold space for you, you'll want to learn how to both *ask* and *enroll* your partner in providing this service to you. As you work with this idea, you'll come to find that honesty with your partner about both when you are able to hold space for them, as well as how much space you can hold will get things off to a more successful start. Of course, you will also want to be considerate of how much space you are asking or assuming your partner can hold for you. In times when you experience heightened emotions or are triggered by old wounds, you may immediately want to tell your partner all about them. Even if you are doing this consciously with the intent of looking at your wounds and triggers for the sole purpose of healing them and not just to vent to your partner, it may be too much for them to take on. Your partner may also be going through a lot of emotional turmoil and it's possible that you're not aware of all of the energy they may be using to hold space for their own issues or stressors.

I've found that it is very honoring and makes for better communication if you learn to enroll your partner in holding space for you. Remember that holding space takes a lot of energy for the spaceholder, so it is more considerate to approach your partner in a loving manner by *asking* them if they can hold space for you. Giving the other person a chance to share with you, whether or not they can hold space for you, can save both people from resentment and emotional explosions. In order for this to work, both people will have to be fairly conscious of their own needs and emotional state at any given time so they can be honest in their answers of what they're able to do for each other. You'll want to be mindful to not make demands for spaceholding on your partner in the form of declarations. "I need a week to myself in order to work out my inner emotions" might seem like a simple statement of your needs, but it does require your partner to hold space for you until you come back to them. If, for example, your partner has already been holding space for you and you declare that you need additional time to yourself, they may find themselves feeling like they were never *asked* to hold the additional space. This can be especially troublesome in times where your partner assumed they were almost done holding space for you and if they are starting to run low on energy. They may be experiencing their own needs for some closeness, comfort, or help from you with family or personal concerns, and the statement that you need additional space might be really pushing them over the edge.

This way of communicating when you need their support allows for your expectations of what they can or will do for you to be formed based on your partner's honest assessment of their ability and not on an assumption you've made. Honoring each other in this way will lead to more defined expectations, clearer communication, and an overall harmonious relationship.

MAKING DECISIONS ON YOUR OWN

When there are big decisions to be made and your aren't sure what is truly in your heart, it's best to put any decision on hold, stop holding space for others, and get into your own space for a while. If you feel as if you don't have the time to take for this process, but you're still unsure as to what you really want to do, remember that many times we may imagine that we have to make a decision more quickly than is really necessary. If you aren't ready yet, see if there is any way that you can buy yourself some time, particularly if it is you who is putting pressure on the immediacy of your decision making.

If after some time you know that a decision is still necessary and it's time to look at things again, try to commit to fully exploring all of your feelings, even if it is only in small doses. The decision you may be faced with may not be one that you'd want to face, or even consider, so be easy on yourself while you're mustering up the courage to confront all of your emotions head on. You'll also want to be completely honest with yourself during this process. Your decision may seem like a raging tiger, looking to devour you if you dare face all there is to see, but know that the tiger is only fear, be brave, and look it in the eye. For more help on this, go back to the introduction and *fear sitting*. When you're ready, go ahead and explore the good feelings, the bad ones, the frightening ones, and the messy ones

If you are having trouble knowing what it is you need to explore to make the decision, try asking yourself and or your benevolent team some questions. Ask about the pros, the cons, and if there are any underlying feelings you may be having about any aspect of the situation. Keep asking questions until you arrive at the deeper reason behind your feelings. Do this for as long as is necessary to get answers.

Another thing you can try when you still don't know the answer is to try putting it to the side and letting go of your direct focus on it. In this way, you're not forgetting about the issue, but it is no longer your primary focus. It remains in your awareness that the issue will need your full focus and attention soon, but until then, it will stay out of the forefront of your mind so that your unconscious may go to work. This can be compared to the phenomenon of getting life's answers or big ideas while using the restroom, taking a shower, or doing the dishes. By doing something else for a while and taking the pressure off, you're holding space for a natural answer or solution to emerge.

You'll want to hold yourself in the highest love during this process as you look at whether your feelings are coming from old patterns and old voices in your head, or if they really do point to something that needs attention in the present moment. Presence, stillness, breathing, asking for assistance from your divine helpers, and blessing yourself with lots of love for your pain and confusion are all very kind things to do for yourself during this process. This will ensure that your final decision will come from purely from love, rather than stem from fear from old triggers or wounds.

After you've held this space for yourself, you'll land upon a place where you can make a step forward from a place of calm and surrender. You'll know it's right because you've landed in a grounded place. You'll embody your decision, not just try it on like a piece of clothing that only fits on the outside. Your decision will live within you. You'll *be* your decision, your decision will *be* you and you'll have stepped upon solid ground and not sand.

After you have gone through this process, you'll realize that what you've done was to allow your authentic self to come to the surface and present itself to the world through your actions. Now, any decision you make will feel grounded and centered and will become a solid foundation on which you can continue to build for years to come.

MAKING DECISIONS WITHIN A PARTNERSHIP, SMALL GROUP, OR FAMILY

When two or more people are trying to reach a decision or agreement, keeping the conversation open is a method that can be used to ensure that everyone gets a fair shake. This method may be used when it is important that all members of the group are on board with the decision and everyone feels honored and fully heard. Examples of when you would want to keep the conversation open would be with partnerships, families, and those with whom you have a personal investment in their happiness and wellbeing.

When a decision needs to be made in a personal partnership or family, there are times when shifting the focus can bring about the desired result. All parties involved in the decision may have different thoughts, feelings, or concerns. In order to truly honor everyone, all parties may need to do their own work, as described in the *making decisions on your own* section, in order to understand their deepest feelings on the subject and to help the group reach the most agreeable decision.

Agreeing to keep the conversation open alerts the other parties that you are not dismissing the issue, but rather that you really do care and wish to take the time not just to come up with a decision, but to find the right one. This method may take a bit longer than just jumping to an answer, but in the end, carefully thought out and organic decisions seem to prove much more sustainable than those forced under a real or imagined deadline. In an equal partnership or family where there is disagreement, this means all parties holding space for each other must put their thoughts into the pot until an organic decision can be reached. Decisions both big and small can benefit from this practice as things will go along much more smoothly when the highest and best decisions are made, even if they take a bit longer. Sometimes this will involve taking a break from the discussion while each person consults their own feelings, and sometimes it will involve sessions with the other members, carefully tossing feelings into the ring in order to get the discussion flowing. It is worth noting that those in your partnership or group who are unfamiliar with spaceholding or who feel pressure to make quick decisions, may not initially accept or embrace this practice. The amount of time it may take them to see the value in this type of communication is certainly variable, but inevitably, all parties will benefit by everyone feeling on board and honored with a decision that has been made truly jointly.

If there are a lot of conflicting feelings and you're having trouble expressing what you need to in order to be truly heard and considered, it is possible that the timing is not right for others to be able to truly hear or hold space for your concerns in that moment. This can be due to their own triggers, stress, tiredness, or perhaps their focus on too many other things at the moment. In this case, a good skill to learn is to ask the other person if they are able to hold space for what you would like to express and if not, when would be a better time to reconvene.

In my work, I've had the pleasure of counseling couples. When one partner has something to say to the other that will bring lots of insight, but is emotionally charged, I'll ask the other partner if they are able to hold it in that moment. They usually give me a confused look. I then explain further, "Can you hold space for what your partner is about to tell you? Can you hear it in an unbiased way and hold yourself at arm's length from any feelings it may normally provoke? Can you create a space to work on this issue, as if it were clay in the middle of the room, and feel that it is not being directed at you?" Asking these questions also seem to lessen any supercharged emotions that the first person feels the need to express. It lets them know that they've been heard and are being given the opportunity to speak.

Approaching a conversation with a *can you hold this right now* approach shows your partner what type of conversation you'd like to have and asks a very honest question of the other partner. This will allow for both of you to find the best timing for the conversation, giving a potentially charged issue the best chance of being dealt with and everyone feeling peaceful and happy about the outcome. Real feelings have the chance to be expressed, and everyone can walk away from the table feeling like they've been respected and given a fair shake. Keeping the conversation open gives people a chance to fully explore feelings and make the decision that feels best for everyone after all core feelings have been considered.

Related to this, I've found this method can also be used when there's something you may want to just throw out there for future notice. It is a way of getting the ball rolling on more difficult conversations that may take a while to flesh out between all of the parties. It's like saying "Hey, I'm just throwing this out there," when you know the timing isn't right for either party to actually get into a discussion. You want to at least inform the other person that you would like to have a conversation about it in the near future. That way, the subject matter isn't a surprise, and they can begin to either work with it or to put it aside for later contemplation.

When the time does come to go back into discussion, using *I* statements to express how you feel is also of the utmost importance. This gives you the best chance to explore your feelings in the energetic container being held by two or more parties in a discussion. If you are talking through your feelings as you're sorting them out, I've even found it best to introduce your statements with, "I don't know exactly how I'm feeling or if this is a trigger of mine or not, but this is what this idea or proposal is bringing up for me."

The other great benefit to these methods is that besides being very honoring to all parties, when two or more people hold this type of space for a conversation where they are sharing true and deep feelings, very often a decision will organically arise out of the space being held. Sometimes one person will come back to the discussion totally on board with the other people as they've had a shift in perspective. Or suddenly you just *know* why you are feeling the way you are and what's behind it. This is much like when people come to their *aha* moments during counseling. No one actually needs to *make* a decision, but rather a decision organically arises out of the space held and the conglomeration of feelings and intentions that were put into it.

Being Present, "Keeping Things on Track," and Shifting
-Performing the Job of Spaceholder in Personal Relationships-

To be a spaceholder, you must have an incredible amount of focus on the present moment. Being present will allow you to keep a good read on the feelings, emotions, and mood of everyone involved and will alert you to the need to adjust your spaceholding tactics if necessary. Learning to be more present can be achieved in many ways. Stillness, quiet, and meditation are a few of the most popular avenues used to learn to cultivate presence. When you hold space for another person, conversation, or situation, you must be perfectly aware of that moment in time in its pure form. There may be distractions and other things going on around you, but as an adept spaceholder, you will have developed as second nature the ability to tune in and lock in on only that which is relevant to the situation at hand. In this way, you'll be able to keep the conversation on track, and *the car on the road*, as I like to put it.

As you become more skilled at being present, you can then add the other elements of spaceholding necessary for a successful conversation, planning session, or decision-making session. The first thing to consider when preparing to hold space for one of these types of situations is to *set the space*. Setting the space is to perform either physical or energetic tasks with the intention of keeping the integrity of the conversation at the highest level. There are as many different ways to intentionally set the space as people have preferences, so find something that feels genuine and authentic to you, and then adjust as necessary. One example for a more personal conversation, planned for the purpose of making a decision on an issue, might be to set the space by stating the intention or goal of the conversation before you begin. Setting the space in this way allows for everyone to energetically align themselves with that goal and to know what the point of the discussion is. In this way, if the discussion begins to veer off topic and you have to pull things back to center, the other participants should at least not be surprised by your actions.

The next skill you'll want to use after you've become very present and set the space if the conversation was planned ahead of time, is to help to keep a conversation or tense situation on track. When you are holding space for yourself and others in personal situations, you are in charge of keeping all the words and ideas that are entered into the conversation in alignment with the goal of the conversation while also allowing things to unfold organically in the space that you've created. Personal conversations where a spaceholder is necessary have a high likelihood of becoming emotional or intense if not kept in check. As you'll want to allow for things that need to be explored without stifling anyone's expression, keeping things on track can simply be a reminder for someone to stay on topic and to ensure that erroneous points won't continue to be made. Keeping things on track can also be a way to keep the intensity of the conversation to a manageable level and of bringing the energy of the conversation back to love when it has veered too far in the other direction. When you keep things on track, you remain present to what may need to be done at any time to maintain the integrity of the energetic container you've created to hold the conversation.

Shifting is another skill that you'll work with often as a spaceholder. Shifting is when the mood of a person or situation changes dramatically from what it was, or when the energetic space that was being held for a particular matter, mood, or emotion has been noticeably dropped or withdrawn. It can be beneficial or non-beneficial when things shift. If you've decided previously to schedule a conversation when the timing seems best, it will also be beneficial in this case to set the space by making sure everyone has *shifted* from what they were previously doing. If people have just been working, driving, or on the phone, allowing them time to shift and give their complete attention to the present moment and conversation will pay dividends. Shifting can also become necessary within the conversation if intense emotions are coming up or being dealt with and the space gets particularly heavy. The participants may be growing weary and not able to stay with the conversation much longer and the overwhelming energy in the room may become palpable. You may even see people moving around in their chairs or beginning to look uncomfortable. In a situation like this, shifting the energy or space that's being held is beneficial to everyone. Alleviating the pressure may better allow for the conversation to stay open and for the issue to be worked on. Being keenly aware of when it's time to shift in or out of heavier or lighter moods and energies will allow communication to flow more easily and fruitfully. The spaceholder's wisdom in when to take a break from a conversation and when to buckle down and dig into the issues at hand will be a tremendous attribute to all parties involved.

SPACEHOLDING IN PERSONAL GROUPS WHERE YOU ARE ALSO A MEMBER

A particularly challenging role for a spaceholder in personal settings is to facilitate groups where you have personal relationships with the participants and to be mindful of those relationships. If you find yourself as both facilitator and member of a group of close friends or peers that does not have a designated leader, I have heard of facilitators who designate a *heart keeper*. This person is charged with the duty of pulling everyone back to the point at hand if things should get off track. This way, the facilitator can keep the worry of impacting personal friendships out of the mix and keep the majority of their focus on the space they're holding or on the information that they're relaying. As spaceholding in these situations does put the facilitator between a rock and a hard place, it is unfair to put the entire burden on that person to try to navigate quality spaceholding duties while keeping their personal relationships with the group members in good standing. If the group needs a facilitator but there's no heart keeper designated to share the duties, then spaceholding/facilitation duties should be rotated among the members at each meeting in order to fairly balance the burden.

When keeping things on track for a friend or family member, your knowledge of their personality, what they will respond to best, and your history with them can help you to consider the best delivery and timing of actions and words necessary to keep things on track. It's a tricky situation anytime you attempt to hold space for those you know and love while simultaneously holding space for yourself, all while keeping your relationship with them a primary focus. Remember in this case that your job is to hold energetic space for the highest outcome to emerge for the person or for your relationship, and do your best to hold yourself to the same standards as the others.

Families, friendships, or partnerships in which there's a strong spaceholder have an advantage over those that do not. This is why spaceholding is such an important and necessary job and why a spaceholder should honor themselves, as well as be acknowledged for their role. If there is no one to keep things on track, it may be harder to bring everyone's energy back to love when problems arise. It is my hope that in bringing attention to and honoring the service that a spaceholder provides in these relationships, a greater sense of worth can be attributed to the spaceholder, and a greater sense of gratitude can be instilled in those who are benefitting from their abilities.

Holding Space for the Dreams of Others

In a world based on cooperation rather than competition, holding space for the highest dreams, creations, and manifestations of others will help you, them, and our planet thrive. When you can allow yourself to be excited and hold space for the highest dreams and creations of those around you, the domino effect this creates and the good feelings and energy that will be cultivated by it can only add to that which *you* wish to create.

Under this idea, it's obvious that the jealousy and hurtful competition that we're sometimes taught as a means to reaching our dreams are of no value. What we have not been taught in our society, which is based on separation rather than inclusion, is that when we lift others ... we lift ourselves. This doesn't mean that we lift others at the exclusion of ourselves, or that we martyr ourselves because that would be using our energy in a counteractive manner as well. What it does mean is that when we spend some of our energy augmenting the dreams and intention of those around us, rather than acting in fear that there isn't enough to go around, we also lift ourselves. We also open the channel of energy for help to come to us from other avenues. Holding space for others' dreams will magnify the energy that they have for their creations and open the flow to the world. This magnification, just like praying for them, will increase two-fold the intention, energy, and focus needed to bring their creations to life. Holding back our energy from others' desired benevolent dreams only serves to harm all of us. If we block their energy, ours is blocked. If we don't extend ourselves to give their dreams our support or energy, we're holding back their manifestations and consequently blocking our own. Just to further the point, if we have anything to gain from this person's success, we're not just hurting them by blocking them, but ourselves as well. When one of us wins, we all win.

If you're finding it hard to support others' dreams or are feeling competitive or envious, you're probably caught in some type of fear with an old trauma or wound. It is also possible that the dreams that others are working towards might be things you'd like to do but think you can't. Either way, holding your energy back from them, or directly opposing them will not get you what you want and will only create more trouble and karma for you. If you're having trouble, it's best to be honest, look inside yourself, and talk to your higher power and/or a counselor. In doing that you can begin to find out what parts of yourself you are suppressing and can begin to cultivate them while you focus on building your own self-worth, self-love, and self-confidence.

When we're cooperating instead of competing, all of our dreams have a chance to come true. Inclusion, rather than exclusion, is the key. Now again, this doesn't mean forgetting about yourself or letting things into your world that are obviously working against you. Rather, believing in and building yourself up enough to know that giving others your love and support will not diminish you, nor will it threaten your ability to manifest. In fact, it can only enhance your ability, if you just believe it. We are all here to complement each other with the unique things we bring to the table. We may not have found the outlet for our talents yet or just the right spot where our puzzle piece fits, but if we keep holding the space for ourselves and others, we can keep our attitudes and spirits high, hold space for each other as we move along on our journeys, and ultimately be shown where we all fit. Holding space for ourselves, our friends, our enemies, and humanity as a whole will get us all there. Indeed, it is a major key to how we can get where we want to go and the reason why I am writing this book—to give attention and focus to this important step in all of our journeys, both together and alone.

Holding Space to Help Someone Become Who They Really Are

You can hold space to help yourself or someone else become who they truly are—to grow into their true and authentic self. Giving someone the room to become themselves is holding the space for their true unfoldment. I have chosen various avenues of homeschooling for my child since second grade. One of the big reasons I chose this route is because I wanted him to become who he really is without any influence on who he *should* be or with any false notions of who he actually is. I wanted someone to hold the space for him to love learning about himself and the world around him. I never wanted learning to be a chore or something he despised or for him to be given a one-size fits all world-view. I wanted him to be able to freely explore all avenues and make his own hypotheses and form his own opinions from there. It's my feeling that to learn is a natural instinct and desire when there's something that you wish to learn about. With all of the access we have these days to information, it no longer seems necessary to confine yourself to a specific curriculum in order to possess the knowledge you need to give yourself the best opportunity to really discover yourself and give your gifts to the world. After I became an entrepreneur many years ago, I think my eyes opened to the joys of following your passion and giving your true gifts to the word instead of following one prescribed path for the options you *think* are available for you. I know school is a viable option for many people and not everyone gets caught inside a box after experiencing it, but I wanted something or someone that could really hold space for him, and until that something better comes along, that something is homeschooling and that someone is me.

In adult relationships that are a good fit for both parties, one partner should be able to allow the other the room to grow, the room to *become*. Holding space and being supportive of letting the other go after their dreams and become who they really are can only increase the love and harmony on the planet. Holding space for each other's expression, unfoldment, personal development, and passions is one of the best gifts we can give. Sometimes we just need to let our partners and friends know that they have our support. Sometimes we need to stand beside them, and sometimes we need to actively do something to assist them when they're trying to reach specific goals. The trick is to pay attention to our partners and friends, sense what type of support or space holding we think they may benefit from and then ask them what they need.

In holding space for ourselves and others to fully become our truest selves, we'll have gifted the world far more than we might be able to with individual acts toward saving the world. In allowing another the space to become their truest self, we have now brought one more person back to their more expansive, authentic, and radiant be-ing, alive with knowing their true freedom and sovereignty. When the majority of us feel that, the planet will have no choice but to reach critical mass and tip the scales towards peace and harmony.

Being There for People When Times are Tough

When hard times, grief, or trauma affect you or those you love, we often hear that it's best to just be there for the person, rather than to do or say anything. There are times when things can be awful and there's nothing that anyone can do or say that will make anyone feel more comfortable. In that case, sometimes the most important thing we can do is to just hold a loving space for ourselves or others while we're going through the rough spots. It's important to feel and process all of the emotions that we need to feel during these times so that nothing is repressed or shoved under the rug, only to emerge again later. It is just as much a part of our life experience to feel these emotions deeply as it is to explore our happy and joyful feelings. Repressing any of them will cause us to have less than a fully lived life as the only way out is *through*. We may not want to feel these emotions or may be uncomfortable being around others' sadness or anger, but the more comfortable we get with feeling our own feelings, the less uncomfortable we'll be around others who are experiencing the same emotions.

Holding space for someone that is experiencing the stronger emotions of grief or shock from tragedy is a separate consideration. It can end up feeling a bit like emergency spaceholding, much like an ambulance and emergency room doctor would do for an emergency physical issue. Nothing very specific is necessarily called for, though at times doing a few tasks for the person may be appropriate. Other than that, you'll just hold them in an energetic container of love while they experience all the emotions that they need to feel. There is no greater act of love than to offer yourself in service to that person with full knowledge that perhaps you alone are keeping them afloat. In this instance, you are holding space for one who cannot do so for themselves and allowing them the full safety of your loving energetic container.

In doing this for another, however, be sure to remember the rule of keeping the energetic container you are holding for them separate from yourself. As well, do not ever allow one in grief to abuse you or the service you are providing. If they begin to act out at you or to take out their anger or frustrations on you in any way, you'll need to bring in a professional or back off until the person can become more conscious of themselves and their actions. Holding the space for someone who is deeply traumatized after a tragedy is a temporary duty. You'd be wise to help them to stand on their own feet again by backing up when appropriate so that they may turn to something greater than themselves. You may also need to refuse to accept projections of their feelings as this will also help them to continue to move forward in a healthy manner and not to fall into an unhealthy pattern of victimhood, blaming, or taking out their feelings on others.

The point of emergency spaceholding is to support the person in need when they're not able to support themselves, just as a doctor or ambulance is called when a physical crisis may render someone unable to care for themselves. When healing has begun, however, the spaceholder or caretaker must know when it's time to offer less carrying and more empowerment by allowing the person to regain their strength and move forward in as healthy a manner as possible. At times, the person who has been supported may offer resistance as they may believe they're not yet ready to handle things on their own. With patience, perseverance, and desire, they will again be able to feel and handle things that they may not think they can.

Grief is grief and needs to be explored fully before it can be released. The one in grief should be careful, however, to not put too much pressure on those who are holding space for them as it *is* a heavy burden to carry. The grieving or angry person is still responsible for feeling and dealing with their heavier emotions either on their own, with their counselor, or higher power. When we hold space for others who are angry or grieving, we do best to allow them their feelings, but not take on or process any of them for them. We're not there to feel their feelings for them, only to love them through the process.

As emergency spaceholding is a caregiving situation, any time you knowingly take on a role of caretaker, be sure you pay close attention to two factors.

1. That your intention is to uplift, support, and hold space, rather than to fix, rescue, or do anything for someone that they are capable of doing and should do for themselves.

2. That you are paying extra attention to make sure your needs are

being taken care of first, that you have enough energy to do the extra spaceholding, and that *you* are the best person for the job—shame and guilt completely aside.

In the Creation Process

At this point in your journey, you've become pretty confident that you are indeed a spaceholder. You realize that you've been using your talents for yourself as well as those you relate to and will continue to do so. Since we are all creative in some way, we all have *creations* that we would like to bring into the world. As a spaceholder, you are especially attuned to how to harness the energy of an open mind and heart to bring in what wants to be born through you. As you create, there are a few things you will need to keep in mind in order to keep yourself in the most open space possible while still taking care of your everyday wants, needs, and loves.

Being in the Bubble- Staying Focused

I've noticed as I have been writing certain portions of this book that I've needed to stay in my own energy, much like having a bubble around myself while I'm in the writing process. I've gone about my daily life between writing, typing, and editing sessions. However, I've largely stayed in the bubble. I've let people around me know that I'm writing and need to stay in my own energy and that while doing so I can't get too involved in other people's energy or issues. My stepping forward and putting myself out there has caused some old beliefs and issues to come forward to try to get my attention. I would almost always dig further and try to find and heal what was coming up. But, my intuition and higher power were guiding me to just stay in my own space and continue to move forward. I acknowledged and know that my action steps were bringing this up, but I retained the feminine energy of holding space for myself, while allowing my *doing* part to continue to move forward.

Any creative endeavor will require this type of focus and spaceholding for ourselves. Creating art, writing a song, or developing a prototype of a new product, all require the focused energy of space held for oneself, and are enhanced when those directly around you can honor or hold any space you may need. Honoring yourself enough to take that space and respecting yourself for what you are birthing are some of the best gifts you can give yourself and greater humanity. What you are birthing may well be one of humanity's greatest gifts, or at least one of your greatest gifts to humanity and those around you. Of course, you will want to maintain proper attention and balance of work, family life, relationships, and other priorities or responsibilities. It's up to each one of us to search our souls to find out what is most important to us and how to give proper attention to each while allowing a little extra for the part of us that may need it.

I believe part of the reason we're on earth is to create and to have the divine express and experiment with creation through us. When we slow down our overly masculine thinking and remove ourselves from our boxes and ideas of what is acceptable and worthy for us to be doing, we allow the space for our gifts and talents to be brought into physical form for the benefit and enjoyment of all humanity.

Giving ourselves time and space during the creative process and being careful to treat ourselves tenderly during this very open and vulnerable creative time is actually a very unselfish thing to do. By taking care of ourselves during this time of sacred birthing, just as a pregnant and laboring mother would take care of and nurture herself during that most vulnerable time, the fruits of our labors are better cared for. In turn, this brings a much better chance of allowing for all types of benefits and perks to be brought to the world through our creation's very existence.

The world absolutely needs people working in the masculine energy of *doing* in order for anything to move forward. However, if we as a society continue to subscribe to the out of balance idea that to do is more important than to be, the artists, philosophers, visionaries, poets, inventors, and musicians may not allow themselves to be in the space needed for new creations.

Holding Space for Your Dreams

Einstein said that the definition of insanity is doing the same thing over and over and expecting different results. Sometimes, when the way appears to be blocked and you just keep running up against the same things, or additional unwanted things, holding space can make all of the difference. While it is possible you may feel as if you are taking a step back, the truth is that the doors you were knocking on were not bringing you what you wanted anyway and sometimes continuing to knock was only making things worse.

There are many reasons why something might not be manifesting for you. Regardless, continuing to push in the same direction or knock on the same doors is only indulging yourself in the definition of insanity. In addition, you're using your energy to fight against something rather than flowing with it as it exists. A better approach is to step back for a moment and take a breather. When doing this, you're not giving up, you're just holding some space for it until it makes sense to move forward again, maybe in a different way, with a different energy, or perhaps with a different intention.

If the dream, idea, or situation you wish to manifest is not one you're easily willing to give up, then it is assumed you'll also be willing to give it the proper time and space it needs to manifest in the highest and best way. It's also possible that the time you take to just hold space for your creation may be filled with other lessons you may need to learn, people you need to meet, or interesting adventures for you to have and grow from. It's even possible that your dream may morph and change, based on who you were and who you may become while you're holding space for it to become manifest. The point is that stepping away from pushing your energy forward in an unhealthy way when things are not flowing does not mean you are giving up or are not as passionate about your dream. Keep dreaming. If it is to be and is for your highest good, your dream has no choice but to come true for you in some way.

Giving yourself some time and space from directing your energy solely to that idea, situation, or person will also free you up to have the other experiences you may need to have first. You may even decide that your dream has changed form a bit, or that you don't even want it anymore. Maybe it will show up in a package that you were not expecting. Maybe you were looking for the feeling behind it, rather than the external circumstances that you imagined would bring it to you. Or, maybe you even had it in front of yourself the whole time but just weren't in a place to notice it yet.

Holding space for your dreams means continuing to dream them. This may not always happen consciously and directly, but involves keeping the flame lit in your soul so that you're allowing yourself to have other experiences while keeping yourself open and flexible along the way. It's also possible that your dreams are so big that many other factors will need to come into play before you'll be able to manifest them in their entirety. There may be lots of other people or situations that have to be put into place before your vision can manifest and there may not be much you can do to hurry that along. In that case, holding space is a great thing to do and may well be the *only* thing you can do.

Holding space means putting something on the back burner in your mind and heart while you get on with other things but keeping it close enough to the front that you're still aware of its presence.

Holding space for your dreams is one of the greatest gifts you can give to yourself and to the world as it involves finding and cultivating your gifts, talents, and desires, and then bringing them forth into the universe in the highest and most brilliant way. You were put here with talents and dreams. Allowing yourself space and time to bring those things into reality in the highest way is one of the biggest things you can do for yourself and the world around you. Stifling yourself, giving up, or thinking you aren't doing enough for your dreams will not help you to move forward any faster.

Knowing and honoring the times when it is a very important part of the process to hold space for yourself and others is a very noble task and is all part of the gestation process. As you look through your life periodically and congratulate yourself for all you've accomplished, remember to include all the times you've held space for yourself and others among the highest of these achievements, for they deserve just as much of your pride and honor.

Holding Space to Allow Your Talents, Passions, and Dreams to Show
Themselves to You

In the last section, I spoke of holding space for your dreams and passions. But what if you don't yet really know your dreams and passions? Well, you could always hold space for and support others while holding the space for yourself to find your unique talents. As I mentioned before, we all have unique attributes, skills, and passions that fit into the puzzle of the greater whole. Just because you may think that you don't have any, or that you don't know what they are, does not mean that they aren't there. If you find yourself in this category, your energy may be best used either in supporting others in their dreams, or taking the time to discover what yours are by allowing yourself to get out of your comfort zone to try new experiences and ideas on for size.

Another idea is that you may have more to learn and more experiences to have before your true life purpose will be revealed. It's also possible that you may need to fill the role of a *do-er* and to affect others by how you show up in what you are *do-ing*. There are many spaceholders whose major talents, skills, and passions are a bit more action oriented, but who affect people through their spaceholding abilities in those types of jobs. They may be found in many different primary roles, but are often secondarily and subtly serving as the company's best facilitator, spaceholder, or customer service agent. There are also those who find themselves shining in more familial or personal roles, such as being the best friend, parent, or caregiver around and who may have already found their life's passion through those roles. If so, holding space for others, while remembering to take the time for themselves, may be this type of person's highest calling.

If none of these situations resonate with you and you still aren't sure what your skills and attributes are or how to best use them, perhaps the best use of your energy is to hold space for yourself. Focus all of your energy only on yourself in order to see clearer, heal something, or to clarify. It's quite possible if you find yourself in this situation that you have some inner work to do, maybe some that you don't even know about. Your life purpose could also be so large that you'll need to go through many different experiences before you can even begin to put them together. Either way, selfishly holding the space for yourself by taking the time for you to find out who *you* are may be the best gift you could give yourself. Spaceholding is a worthy and important activity no matter who you are doing it for, most *especially for yourself.*

Manifesting Your Destiny

Now that you better understand how to care for yourself as you create, you begin to become more excited to create the kind of life you've always dreamed of for yourself and those around you. You've come to realize that if you can hold space for your creations, you can certainly take that even further to create the kind of life and environment that you want. And thus begins your journey into holding space for yourself for the purpose of manifesting your dreams and goals.

*Holding Space for Love, Money, or Anything Else You Wish to Manifest Using the **Law of Attraction** in Spaceholding*

Whether you wish to manifest a new or improved love relationship, more money, a new house, new career, or anything else, using a combination of holding space, asking your higher power for assistance, and getting yourself aligned with your true desire via the Law of Attraction, can help you to attract what you are looking for. Whether you believe in God, Science, the Law of Attraction, or all of them, you can start by asking for what you want, and then do your part to just hold space for it and relax your energy surrounding it. During the time you are holding space, begin to notice if there are any parts of you that may be resisting letting the things you want into your life, and if there are any, work on clearing those while you wait. If you have a blockage, consciously or unconsciously, to receiving what you want, according to the Law of Attraction, it will be virtually impossible for what you want to get past that blockage. Likewise, if you are angry, complaining, frustrated, or consistently seeing yourself as a victim, it will be hard for you to receive anything new from the universe. If you are too busy focusing on what you *lack*, or if you're angry that you *don't have*, you won't be able to let it in. The definition of the Law of Attraction goes something like this: "Like attracts like. You get what you put your energy and focus on, whether wanted or unwanted, and what you desire, desires you." Be sure to focus your energy on what you *do* want, and then work on surrendering, and believing that you are worthy of having it.

When you are working on manifesting something you desire, remember to also be aware of the old adage, "Be careful what you wish for." This is where you may want to lean upon your higher power for guidance. Some good ways to do this when asking for what you desire are to:

—Be very clear about what you are asking for
—Be a bit more general about what you are asking for
—Ask for things that will get you to the *feeling* you desire
—Ask for what you think you want

Then add, "Or that which is for my highest good," to your request. This way, if you are out of alignment with being able to attract your true desire, or if it is not what is best for you, your higher power can guide you in ways to either come into alignment with your desire, or to lead you towards things that are more aligned with your highest good.

To further illustrate this point, many times when we think we want a certain thing, what we are focused on may not actually be what we truly desire. Rather, we are looking for the *feeling* we think we will have when we obtain it. We also may think we want something, but don't realize that if it's not lining up yet, maybe something even better, something that we can't even fathom, is waiting for us somewhere down the line. Holding space for the big things we want consists not of trying too hard to find them or make them happen, but by just holding them in our hearts, without squeezing the life out of them, or trying too hard to control them. Big things often take time to properly unfold as many pieces may need to be put into place. Rushing them may not bring us the sustainable results we may be seeking. Certain things in life just can't be forced or controlled. It's also possible that our higher power may have an even better plan for us or some experiences we must go through first in order to make the things we want turn out in the highest way possible.

Working with your higher power and holding space to manifest your desires can bring up any trust issues you may still have lingering in your psyche. If you fear that you cannot trust anyone or anything but yourself, you'll have a very hard time using the combination of all three things and would be better off concentrating only on the Law of

Attraction. Do what you can to get yourself in vibrational alignment with your desire, clear any blocks you may have to letting it in, and trust that what you desire is indeed what is best for you.

Working with your higher power, holding space, and the Law of Attraction will require a willingness to surrender to something higher and bigger than you, and then trust it to either bring you what is best for your path and growth cycle, open you up to experiences which will help get you in vibrational alignment with your desires, or both. I once asked God to help me be the best counselor I could be. The part of my life that followed consisted of many personal challenges. While these were not necessarily what I thought I desired, they were certainly helping me to gain wisdom on things I'd be using to help the clients who were attracted to my energy and practice in the future. The path of trusting your higher power to bring you your desires requires you to hold space by being willing to focus on what you want, then releasing it to your higher power or the universe to decide how and when to bring it to you. As demonstrated by my example above, when you do ask, be prepared to accept whatever experiences you may be given in order to help you get vibrationally closer to your goal.

When consciously working the Law of Attraction, you must believe that you can have what it is that you desire. If you do not believe that you can have it, you may unconsciously want to prove yourself right and then will not be able to allow it to be brought into your life. This is where adding a spiritual and personal growth practice and/or a relationship with your higher power can help. If so far you have been able to manifest everything you want on your own, you probably don't have many blocks, or you have a great understanding of how the Law of Attraction works. If your method is working, feels great, and isn't hurting anyone, then by all means keep using it. However, if you ever find yourself dreaming of something bigger that you can't seem to get to on your own, instead of pushing, try asking for what you desire, thinking about it, feeling it, imagining it, drawing a picture of it and then letting it go. Letting go doesn't mean you've given up or don't want it anymore, it just means letting go of your attachment to how or when it will show up. We can push and work very hard to make things happen the way we think they should, but at some point in our lives, that method may either stop working, or we may realize that we are not always getting what we *truly* desire by doing it this way. To truly dream big, surrender and trust that something larger than you can help you manifest more than you could ever manifest on your own. There's no way for you to know all of the workings of the universe at any given time and how they can best be manipulated to help get you what you want in the best and highest way.

If you can cultivate the patience and trust to wait for what you truly desire, you are not giving up your dreams or failing to recognize your opportunities, you are just holding space, resting in the knowing that you are worthy and deserving of what it is that you desire, and you are willing to wait for it to be brought to you in all of its glory. If you notice that you have been brought something that is *almost* what you desire, then there is almost certainly something even better in store for you in the not too distant future. Having the patience to hold space for what is really desired can save you from *settling* or giving up too soon. Further, loving ourselves enough to wait for what we really want can also bring things to us quicker, as loving ourselves always puts us in a better place to receive.

Working Smarter and Not Harder — Getting Out of Your Own Way

As discussed earlier, the way of nature is to impregnate, gestate, and birth ideas in the container of the feminine energy of *be-ing* and then for the masculine energy of *do-ing* to take them out into the world. If you follow that guidepost, you will not feel the need to push too hard or force your creations into being before they have had time to properly gestate. What I mean by this is that your grand ideas involving life purpose, big changes, and big dreams are all seeded in the feminine energies first. These big dreams and ideas need the help of many different forces, energies, and people to be able to be brought into full manifestation. If you worry that you aren't working on it hard enough or going fast enough, you may be putting just enough pressure on it to get it stuck in neutral. Since we are given divine ideas in a divine space, you should remember to honor them by doing your very best to assist them in becoming fully manifest. And sometimes, contrary to current

Western methods of thinking, the best way to do that is to move out of the way and do nothing while the universe and your divine helpers are busy putting things into place.

Since we will usually have a sort of amnesia about our life path until we discover what was in us all along, chances are that whatever you might come up with to help you push your divine ideas into manifestation may be futile and even moving you in completely the opposite direction. You must develop trust and faith that your divine ideas are being worked on even when it appears that nothing is moving forward, or things seem to be moving backwards. If you continue to hold space for these ideas in your mind, body, and heart, you can be assured that your divine helpers **are** working to make them happen.

So how do you know if you should be working on something or waiting patiently and keeping yourself busy with other things until you're given the green light? I've found that when you have that question, relaxing and breathing, and not doing anything rash seems to work out for the best. Of course, working with your divine helpers is again of great benefit. As you do that, just remember that you and they are a team. If you are feeling guided toward something that doesn't feel right, ask them about it. Sometimes, you are being tested to find out whether you are in true partnership with them or whether you are taking the lead or the backseat. You can wait for their helpful guidance, but you should always test things against your own heart.

So what happens then when you are given the action steps for what you are aligned with? You jump, of course! The path to further action steps will most certainly open up once you've made the leap. This is how to work smarter and not harder when you're interested in living out your dreams and finding your life's purpose. If you are not interested in focusing on your dreams or life purpose at any given time, know that this is okay, too. You may need to rest, have some other experiences, or just hold space for yourself. We take many of these detours in life while we are further refining our journey to our true path, sometimes even just to turn off our minds or play and that is perfectly healthy.

Though we've been told over and over again by our society that people who have achieved their goals and dreams have gotten where they are with hard work and determination, we may not have fully understood what this truly meant. So let's try shifting the focus. Consider thinking of *determination* as always keeping your dream by your side and in your awareness, and *hard work* as the energy it takes both to hold space and not act as well as specific action steps. Remember, holding space is work, and it does require energy. Certain people's dreams may have contained more action steps, or more space holding, or faith holding than others. Everyone's journey is unique and no one ever achieves their dreams, goals, or life purpose, or walks their journey in the same way. In fact, when you allow your own unique path to unfold, it's possible for you to find out that the goals and dreams you thought you had are not actually your highest dreams and goals. Maybe you thought you wanted the expensive car, but what you really wanted was financial freedom. Maybe you thought you wanted to live in Italy, but what you really wanted was the warm feelings of family, food, and connection that you didn't even realize you associated that with.

Also, be willing to consider that the dream you have may not be as big as the one you're capable of having. In that case, be willing to surrender to the empty space you may sometimes need to hold in order to allow that greater thing to come through for you. Our dreams may be mighty, but sometimes they just aren't mighty enough!

Holding Space for Your Body, Mind, and Spirit, After You Take a Big Step
Forward
The Healing Crisis

Whenever you make a big shift, whether you have begun to dig through some of your layers in order to heal, or have stepped out of your comfort zone or previous patterns, you will inevitably shift the state of being that you were previously in. For example, if you decide to do some healing by working with a counselor, life coach, or healer, you'll begin to loosen up many areas of stuck energy in your body, mind, and spirit. Sometimes when you commit to doing this work and take the first few steps, you may suddenly become ill, develop strange symptoms, or seem to be going backward. Remember in those times that you are doing something drastically different than what you have done, and your entire being may get shaken up a bit as you begin to scrape off the newer layers to expose what's underneath. This is called a healing crisis, and it is part of the process.

A good stillness and inner peace practice, as well as an established relationship with your divine helpers, will help you to understand and be aware of what you are going through so you can best hold space for yourself as you go through it. However, if you've already done some healing work and you did not have those practices in place yet, know that there is no cause for concern. Just be aware that it is possible that you will go through a healing crisis, take good care to hold space for yourself as you go through it and begin to build up your support team so you'll have it in place for the next time.

You may also have to hold space for yourself during potential resistance or backlash when you are taking big action steps forward or outside of your comfort zone. Your ego-self wants to keep you safe and it may not approve of you going out so far beyond what you have been used to. Often, when you are holding space for a big dream and taking any size action steps toward your life purpose, you might feel as if you are suddenly confused or that nothing around you seems to be adding up or making any sense. If this happens to you, do not make any knee jerk decisions in either direction or react too fiercely. Remember to hold space for yourself and breathe through any of the times that things aren't making sense. These things may just be resistance, and they most likely will pass after a while.

If you've practiced centering yourself, breathing, and talking to your divine helpers, you should be a lot more grounded and able to have a firm knowledge about which things you can make decisions about and which things you may need to put aside until the resistance and chaos slow down. You may also feel the desire to check in with a counselor, coach, bodyworker, or energy healer on whether or not you're on track and what's coming up for you. Again, it's best to follow your intuition on these decisions. Remember that during these turbulent times, when your ego-self is fighting hard against your new choices, you may have trouble tuning into your guidance. There's no cause for alarm. Try slowing down, centering, doing some grounding activities and just taking a little time for stillness until you can tune in again with more ease.

It is best to know ahead of time that you are not necessarily on the wrong path if things initially seem to be getting worse instead of better when you begin these programs and that the *healing crisis* is a perfectly normal part of the journey.

Holding Space for Yourself and Keeping Yourself Comfortable:
While You Wait, When You're Weary, or When You're Almost There

The final stretch, after you've worked on something a really long time, can be really daunting. You're tired, you think you've done enough, but things haven't quite shifted yet. You may be getting frustrated, impatient, or feel you're being poked by things that haven't bothered you for some time. What's going on, and what can you do about it?

You're being tested and you need to be highly observant of everything that you're feeling and all that's going on. Time to breathe deep, slow down, and rest. At this point, hurrying to try to *get* the rest of the lessons will just be using your energy in the wrong direction and will make you more frustrated with the pressure you'll be putting on yourself. You might be better off becoming observant and committed to taking everything in, but not vowing to tip the scales while the energy around you feels so strong. You may feel like it's been long enough and you want *action now*, but jumping the gun right before the final result will not bring you the results you seek. Know that it's perfectly okay to feel anxious and ready to go, but that if you act during that energy, you may push things a direction other than the one you desire. Remember, it's not *you* that makes things happen. Your impatience is most likely due to the fact that you can feel how close you are to your goal and you know it's coming soon. There may just be a few more things that need to fall into place and a lot of them you may have no control over. In order to hold space for yourself during this time, it's best if you don't give up. This will give things the best chance of working out and will keep you from potentially tipping the scales too early by forcing your hand and propelling you forward.

During this time, you can also learn a lot about yourself and your feelings by journaling, asking yourself questions, and creating art of any kind to get out all the feelings that may be coming up to help you sort through them. It's a great time to be creative, move your body around, get out in nature, sit with yourself and your feelings, or just play. You don't necessarily need to work hard on revealing your feelings or trying to force anything to rise to the surface, but just be still and feel them. You should also check in with yourself or your spiritual team to see what it is that you're being guided to.

When you're tired, feeling doubt, or feeling weary, holding space for yourself can be as simple as making it okay that you are feeling these things. If you hold your head too high, you might be by-passing the things you need to acknowledge in order to keep yourself healthy and balanced. Sometimes, all you need is to acknowledge that you're growing tired from the journey and that you'd like some relief. Holding space for where you are makes all the parts of your journey okay—the highs, the lows, and the everyday. Being able to let yourself off the hook for not being as optimistic as usual may be exactly what you need to get flowing again. You may also need to get angry for a little bit. Holding space is all about allowing—allowing your thoughts and allowing yourself human emotions—and not feeling as if you have to be perfect. Give yourself permission to throw a small tantrum if it will help, and then get back up and get on the horse. Your life journey cannot always be in forward motion.

Sometimes hanging out, relaxing, silliness, and just *being* are quite appropriate. Allow yourself the breathers and have some fun! Personal growth may be serious business, but it's not *that* serious. If you are not balancing your work with fun, you're missing an important piece of the reason you're here—to learn, grow, explore, laugh, cry, love, and to enjoy every minute of all of it for the deep experience it gives you. If you can't take a break to laugh or to nourish your soul with joy, beauty, or just pure silliness, remember that taking the time to do that is as important as spaceholding to both your and humanity's well-being. It is never a waste or your precious time to be present and partake of those things that bring pleasure to your soul.

Things don't always turn out like we might have expected. Life takes many twists and turns and things that seem like the right answer sometimes aren't, and vice versa. We get the opportunity to learn in a myriad of ways and then to choose which way we prefer. All of the ways are always available to us, but it's up to us to choose the way that we feel is right in every moment. Sometimes we may want to sit back and observe. Sometimes we may want to take a more active role. We can paddle or coast at will, and we will do both all throughout our lives. Remembering *why* we're doing something can make our lives much more relaxed and enjoyable. Sometimes we row the boat, sometimes we are the boat, and sometimes we become the water that moves the boat. When we can surrender to the flow, we can enjoy the ride whether it's up, down, through the rapids, or on calm waters. When things get uncomfortable, we must remember to breathe and hold space for ourselves and the situation and learn and grow from all of our experiences, whether comfortable or uncomfortable.

Though that may seem very serious and full of pressure, we would also do best to think of life as a game. We will inevitably win some, and we will lose some, but the point of playing is in the journey and the fun we have while getting to the end of that particular chapter. Sing, dance, laugh, play, rest, be silly and go with the flow—and make one of your important spaceholding jobs—to hold the space for you to *enjoy* your life.

Letting Go

Sometimes, when you've held space for something for a long enough time and the door hasn't opened, the time might be right to just let go and allow the new to come in. You do not have to let go of the love or the lessons, or what the person or situation meant to you or did for you, just let go of holding space for it. It's also healthy to let go of holding space for something to be the way you want it to if it hasn't ever shown up that way. Letting go is a very healthy thing to do. We all need to periodically clean our homes, closets, wardrobes, minds, and inner house. We go in there and pick out what is no longer serving us that is taking up prime real estate in our hearts, homes, or minds in a positive, constructive way. It is very much a normal part of life to let go of our *attachments* to things, places, and people, so that we may move forward, and move on, allowing in all of the new goodness. By continuing to hold on to those things that are weighing us down, we block ourselves from moving forward into our full abundance in our mind, body, and spirit. Doing a thorough clean-up will clear our hearts, bodies, and minds of the heavy energy that is no longer needed in our lives. It will allow both ourselves and the other party, if it is a relationship with them that we are letting go of, to be free to move on to the next phase of our lives.

We may want to hold on, afraid that we are not honoring our relationships with these people or things, or that we have given up if we let go, but that's simply not true. If we let go in love and gratitude for all that the relationship or situation has brought us, we have made a very big and positive deposit into the universe, and everything and everyone around us will benefit.

When we realize that we've held space for something for a very long time, at some point we realize that we just can't carry all of it anymore. We need to let it go so we can move on to what is next for us and those around us. Letting go of *what was, what could have been*, or *what will be*, is an act of great courage and strength. But as we release our ropes from the shore, our boats are now free to explore all that exists as our new life and adventures await us.

Sometimes holding space means simply loving someone or something and letting go of your desire for them. In this way, you are no longer even holding space but have now truly transformed into being the essence of pure love at its core.

Spaceholding as a Profession

You might come to realize that your talents in spaceholding could be very useful to others in a professional setting. It is then that you may want to consider some of the following information on spaceholding as a profession.

Being Present, "Keeping Things on Track," and Shifting
As a Professional Spaceholder

To be a spaceholder, you must have an incredible amount of focus on the present moment as well as the ability to help people shift, and to *keep things on track*. Employing these techniques when you are holding space for people in personal situations is important, but employing them when you are serving as a professional spaceholder is *extremely* important.

If you are holding space professionally, as a counselor, coach, or group leader, spaceholding requires that you are able to be present by being silent and letting things unfold on their own. You will also need to know the right things to say and possess the correct energy for pulling things back in when they may get off track. This must be done carefully and confidently in order for those that you are leading to trust you enough to lead them towards their highest outcome.

This is where setting the tone for the conversation or event at the start is very helpful. If the timing is right and you have some set-up time before your action will be carried out, creating space by setting the mood or tone can also help to provide the best possible outcome for your experience. Manipulating your environment in this way can involve such things as energetically preparing the space, using purposeful lighting, mindfully ordering events and flow, and creating ambiance. Preparing the space ahead of time increases your ability to hold space for large crowds of people and for you to remain very present to the energy of the group at all times. If you are not able to manipulate the environment ahead of time, at least plan to arrive a bit early to get the feel of the environment that others have set before you begin your duties. Getting familiar with and inserting yourself gracefully into the energy of the pre-set environment and space will pay off in dividends when you are able to command that space with more ease, flow, and grace.

If you are allowed to prepare ahead of time, you should also be mindful of what is planned for the space. If there is anything that could likely cause tension or distraction from the moment, you should plan for things that will help everyone to maintain their presence as well as the purity of the moment. A professional spaceholder should be skilled in knowing how to minimize distractions, how to get everyone on track quickly, and how to easily transition to the next mood or matter at hand. If you are not allowed to prepare ahead of time, you must be very adaptable and able to quickly improvise how to continue to hold or direct the energy of the group for everyone's highest good.

Another way to set the space is to make sure people are aware of the intention and/or goal of the meeting, discussion, or workshop. If people are going to be allowed to speak freely, a safe space must be created at the beginning in order for the room to be able to take that. If people overstep the parameters or are *hogging the space*, you, as the spaceholder, will have to be okay with reining them in and not worry about whether or not they'll like you afterward. Your job is not for them to like you. Your job is to command the respect of all of those that you are facilitating or leading by keeping all of the energy on course and in check. You are the spaceholder, and if you've set the space appropriately from the beginning, no one should challenge you on that. In fact, if you are showing up in your full brilliance as a master spaceholder, you should garner respect both for the space you are holding and for yourself, whether or not someone likes you on a personal level outside of that space.

When you're ready with how the space should look, feel and sound, attention should be paid to how to prepare yourself to transition into the space that has been intentionally created. *Shifting* is another skill that spaceholders will work with often. Shifting is when the mood changes dramatically or when the energetic space that was being held for a particular matter, mood, or emotion has been noticeably dropped or withdrawn. Before holding space for any group or gathering, it's always best to shift out of where you just came from (traffic, work, home, etc.) and into the new space in order to allow for the best results. You may want to meditate, pray, breathe, or do some sort of shifting exercise in order to put yourself in the proper energy to perform your spaceholding duties. Remember that while it's important for *you* to shift yourself from what you may have been doing previously, you'll need to help those that you are holding space for to shift as well. In times when people must abruptly transition from whatever they were doing, knowing how to ease the transition is also an important skill. A good spaceholder always knows that it's more effective, whenever possible, to prepare people for a shift in their current space than to abruptly change the mood or space that is currently being held. As long as it is possible, it is always gentler on our adrenal system and stress reactors to shift ourselves consciously and gently, rather than shockingly or abruptly. These above-mentioned types of shifts are natural, can be conscious or unconscious, and happen often when we go in and out of different activities or energies.

There is another type of shift, however, that may occur during the event or gathering that is not as natural or welcomed as the shifts we make when we begin and end the gathering. These types of shifts can come prematurely. If they do, something that may or should have had the opportunity to come forth in the space may not have been allowed to emerge due to that shift. Examples of this could include an unexpected noise or situation occurring during the event, a person with a particularly large personality attempting to command the room's energy, or someone who is having a particularly hard time and just can't hold it anymore. In these cases, and with time and practice, a professional spaceholder will exude the energy, poise, and confidence to command a room and overly heavy moods, disruptions, or premature shifts will be attended to with ease if they occur. A professional spaceholder is adept at reading the energy of the crowd and knows how to flow with it throughout the event to provide the best experience possible.

In order to obtain positive results and keep things moving forward in a healthy and positive direction, as the facilitator, you must constantly be monitoring the energy of the meeting or gathering. You can hone this skill by continuously doing your own personal growth work and by practicing your trade repeatedly. It helps when you have worked on your issues and triggers and have developed enough self-love that you will not be fearful of how people perceive you when you need to do your job. If you are skilled in this area, you'll have the confidence and the tact to firmly and gracefully hold the space even when you may need to re-direct the energy of the conversation or situation to reclaim the integrity of the space.

To further illustrate this section, I've provided a few examples from my professional spaceholding experiences.

When I perform wedding ceremonies or offer public speaking engagements, I always read the energy of the crowd to measure what tone I should take with my presentation. During a wedding, if a bride or groom is looking very tense and uptight and I know they would welcome it, I may offer a small quip just to get them to smile and breathe again. If I know from previous experience with them that they are a very serious and solemn couple, I'll try something more appropriate if I can feel that they need to lighten up. I'll also use this tactic when working with unexpected occurrences during a wedding or other presentation. Again, if the crowd can take it, I'll offer an appropriate joke that turns the annoyance into a positive and that often helps everyone to feel as if it was a welcome distraction, rather than a nuisance. I've explained airplanes flying over during inopportune times as the couple's personal *congratulatory flyover* and sudden sharp gusts of wind as the heavens or other ethereal realm's statement of approval.

In my spiritual counseling and holistic life coaching sessions, I always remain present to the moment to be able to properly support my clients. Sensing what is coming up for them, how much they can handle, and how to ask appropriate questions that will facilitate a gentle uncovering of their core issues is a key component of my success. *Throwing them in the water* when they can't swim is not always the best approach. Being tuned in to what pace and style will work helps them to celebrate little achievements and to continue forward in a positive direction. I may also need to ramp up my spaceholding in times when I can sense that my client is getting agitated, but I know that they'll be okay and that they'll get big results from sticking with the matter at hand. What I realize in these situations is that all the person needs is a slightly stronger energetic container from me to hold until they can come out on the other side.

In all professional groups, a strong spaceholder and facilitator provide a leading edge as the group will have a much stronger chance of success with someone who is skilled in that role. This is why spaceholding is such an important and necessary job and why spaceholders should be honored and not taken for granted. And yet, because spaceholding as a concept is still widely unexamined, spaceholders may not receive nearly enough recognition for the very essential service that they are providing. If there is no one to keep things on track, productivity is never what it could be. Professional and non-professional spaceholders and facilitators, therefore, should be brought into the light, acknowledged, and their services named, so as to focus and grow this very important aspect of our families, society, and the world. As long as there are differences in people, there will always be differences in opinion. Therefore, in order to move forward with any ideas or solutions gestated in a group setting, someone to keep things on track in a group when a melting pot of ideas and opinions arise is both helpful and necessary and will continue to help us to bring forth wonderful new creations for generations to come.

Ceremonies/Rituals/Rites of Passage and Holding Space

Although American culture has significantly fewer rituals and rites of passage than other cultures, we do have our rituals. Many are religious, but for the purposes of this book, I'll touch on our most common societal rituals. Some of our culture's rituals and rites of passages are celebrated in more of a party atmosphere and without much of a ceremonial aspect: birthday parties, bridal and baby showers, anniversary parties, etc. However, in order to more easily illustrate how holding space applies in ritual and rite of passage situations, I will focus mostly on ceremonial rites of passage here.

Whether it's a graduation, wedding, or funeral, the ceremony is the core of the experience. People may think that they were there only for the party or food, but the truth is that the ceremony is a major marker and influence on the events of one's life. Too often, not enough attention is paid to the facilitation of these major mood shifting life events. Instead, attention is paid to planning the party or food and social aspect of the event, rather than to the consideration of who will be leading, facilitating, and holding space for the ritual or rite of passage. If careful consideration is not made to the choosing of that person, the most important job of holding space for the very important moment might be given to someone who is just not that good at it.

A poorly skilled spaceholder and facilitator may cause everyone to tune out, to experience inner tension or conflict, or they may bore everyone to tears. Just as a great artist or entertainer will capture their audience and take them on an adventure or journey, the facilitator and spaceholder of these special moments have the responsibility of holding the energetic container for everyone present and providing the experience that will most accurately capture the mood, feel, and purpose of the occasion. That person should be an eloquent public speaker, as well as possess enough energy, character, wit, humor, and compassion to adapt at any moment to wherever the energy of the moment might flow. They should be a person with whom everyone in the room can feel comfortable enough to let down their guard for and to allow the experience and energy of the moment to permeate their souls through the spaceholder's words, energy, and facilitation. Whether it is a wedding, funeral, or graduation, not just any person can get up and deliver a heartfelt speech, perfect for the moment.

Just as any large or important project has a leader, general manager, director, or event planner, it's just as important for those planning a ceremonial rite of passage to choose an overseeing spaceholder or facilitator to direct and manage the overall energetic and emotional portion of the event. This is so important because the ceremony and ritual are where major defining moments of life are recorded in one's soul for the person(s) of honor, as well as the invitees. Spaceholders, officiants, keynote speakers, and celebrants are the people who set the tone for the entire experience which illustrates the honored position and service that a spaceholder can provide on a larger, more public scale. If you serve in one of these roles, or will at some point in your life, there is yet another reason to honor yourself for all of your *being* that is the spiritual weightlifting required to sculpt you into a great spaceholder and to resist society's idea that you are not actually *doing* anything.

Counselors/Therapists/Life Coaches/Clergy

Another area where spaceholding is done professionally is seen through the work of counselors, therapists, life coaches, and clergy.

Though our society has unfairly propagated the idea that therapy, coaching, and counseling are only to be used when you are in extreme emotional anguish or dire straits, the services provided by these professional spaceholders can assist you in all seasons of your life. What these professionals provide is an unbiased, professional, and outside perspective on whatever issue you may have that you'd like addressed or to have space held for. Working with a counselor, therapist, clergyperson, or coach either preventatively, or when issues are still small, are the best times to work on your personal growth. By the time a crisis or dire strait situation occurs, a heftier program, similar to a detox, may be needed to help ease the inflamed issues before even attempting to get anywhere near the root causes of the symptoms. Furthermore, looking at and processing your unhealthy patterns and habits and healing your wounds preventatively when you are not in crises, is a lot less stressful, more fun, and can save you much heartache later.

In a holistic lifestyle, focus is given to the mind, body, and spirit as a whole and includes a good balance of our masculine and feminine natures. Though we as a larger society are turning more to a holistic lifestyle, in general, we are still quite out of balance and not very present to ourselves or others. Thus, one of the areas I believe we need the most help in is learning how to relate to ourselves and others. Personal growth, spiritual pursuits (apart from religion), and inner reflection are still seen by many as *woo-woo* or uncool and not something to be embarked upon by those who have any ounce of pride. Spirit in Western society for the average citizen is many times only socially acceptable to access through religion. However, as religion in many cases leans on a more masculine approach to the feminine nature of spirit, many are turning to spirituality without the religion as a way to try to mend the masculine/feminine split.

As a rule, Westernized children are not growing up truly learning how to relate, own their stuff, or heal their emotional or spiritual wounds. In educational curriculum, the art and science of *relating* are not really something that is focused on. Once you've learned your ABCs and 123s, algebra and biology, you are left out in the cold as to how to handle getting into, navigating, and sometimes having to leave relationships. As an adult, you may have no idea what is healthy and what is not, or what is a normal relationship pattern that is no cause for our concern, and what is not. You may not know what to expect from others or from yourself. If the family you grew up in didn't model healthy behaviors within relationships, you might not necessarily even have recognized they were unhealthy since you would have thought your home-life was normal. Even if your gut told you that something wasn't quite right with how things were dealt with in your household, you may have lacked the awareness to even think to seek out the existence of other models of behavior.

Where do you turn as an adult when you inevitably end up frustrated and confused as to why you keep coming up against the same issues, why you're not happy, or why relationships may not be working out as you envisioned? It seems that when it comes down to it, most people value their relationships as the parts of their lives that really mean the most to them. But what do you do and where you go to learn how to truly relate to yourself and others in a healthy way? Honestly, those who embark on a personal growth path or want to learn how to relate better seem to either just stumble upon it or seek it out due to desperation born from problems or issues. It is then that they discover that there is a whole other world out there filled with counselors, pastoral therapists, life coaches, personal growth and self-help books, seminars, and more. If you are able to finally get over the conditioning that steers you away from seeking help for your relational issues, you may just find some answers on how to relate in a healthy manner. No matter how self-aware we are, we all have our own issues, and it is always hardest to see the whole from the parts. Having a professional, caring, and competent spaceholder can be a very handy tool for providing a fresh perspective. A person in one of these fields, if they are doing their job appropriately, can hold the space for you as they *lead you back to yourself* in order to find your strength and answers within.

So many in our society, especially many men as it has not been as allowable for them to access their feminine sides, have been given the understanding that they should already be able to do or handle things themselves. But the truth is, you can only go so far alone. Help from a higher power or some benevolent force that is greater than you, along with a talented counselor, coach, mentor, teacher, or guide, will always get you further. The most skilled of these are the ones who understand how to gently point you in the right direction while holding the space open for you to discover what secrets are just waiting to be revealed.

The professional spaceholder does not necessarily give you advice nor tell you what to do, but rather is highly skilled in being able to pick up on what you are not saying, your mannerisms, your tone of voice, etc., when expressing yourself on a particular subject. They will intuitively know the right questions to ask, how to hold steady if you begin to squirm or get defensive, and how to hold you safe in that moment until you see what you need to see in order to move forward.

Great coaches, counselors, therapists, and clergy are there to support and hold space in an unbiased way. They gain nothing from the life choices of others except the satisfaction of seeing them thrive as they become their most radiant and authentic self. Their truest desire is to help uncover what is absolutely best in every moment.

The Wisdom Keepers and the Activists

THE WISDOM KEEPERS

There are people among us, separate from our mainstream, overly masculine energized world, who are doing a very important job for all of us right now. Certain members of indigenous cultures, sages, healers, evolutionaries, and all types of energetically tuned in people are holding space for our entire planet, in every moment. These people are the energetic guardians of the frequencies of love, peace, harmony, and light on our earth. They may not be well-known, have their names in history books, or get any recognition for the service that they are providing, but know that those who hold the frequency of light and love on our planet are very important. The fact that our society does not widely recognize them is similar to when we don't stop to consider the amount of work that has been done by those who bring us the food we eat every day or provide the clothes we wear. If these people didn't provide that service, we would certainly be lacking a major aspect of our daily lives. What the wisdom keepers do is obviously more subtle, which again points to the passion I have in getting this book out to the world, so that the wisdom keepers can honor themselves for what they do and so others will begin to pay attention to the service that they provide us so overall energetic balance can be restored.

These wisdom keepers understand the energetic history of our existence and their clear and focused presence contributes to the light and energy karma we have as a collective species. They practice the art of being present at all times and are just as toned spiritually as most athletes are physically and scholars and researchers are mentally. They are in tune with nature and the natural rhythm of everything in our existence. Their attention to keeping their own energetic vessel clean, their own self-growth, and their assistance to those around them helps to uplift the collective and make it possible for more people to awaken to their true spiritual natures. We need those who are true wisdom keepers to recognize themselves if their path has not yet been revealed and then to trust their path, no matter what others may have told them. These *be-ers* are contributing every bit as much as the *do-ers* of society. Again, we need both sides to do their jobs and allow themselves to shine to their fullest capacity, for all of us to truly thrive.

Understand also that these wisdom keepers are not just from indigenous cultures, sequestered out in the woods or jungle, completely cut off from the rest of society. Wisdom keepers are everywhere. In fact, those of you who find yourselves in industrial or westernized societies may have an even tougher time on your path as this culture does not teach nor recognize or desire that you cultivate these abilities. Take heart, though, many more teachers, counselors, and sages are now revealing themselves and if you are searching for something more and higher and haven't found it yet, be assured that it is out there and that you will when the timing is right for you. The planet needs people from all parts of the globe to rise up and embody something greater in order for us all to be lifted from the heavier energies of duality and begin to more completely experience a cooperative world in harmony with nature and natural laws, where we all thrive. So if you think you were born into the wrong 'tribe,' you were not, you are needed in your full brilliance at this time, as a teacher, beacon, and lifter of energetic frequency for all of us, and you were probably born where you were for a very specific reason.

THE ACTIVISTS

Activists are the people who are moving forward with action steps on issues that they are also holding space for and would very much like to see resolved. A person who has a particular soft spot or passion for a certain struggle or issue on the global stage may find themselves, through word or deed, emerging as an activist. Whatever level they emerge on, whether they're attending rallies and marching on the government plaza, signing petitions and calling representatives, attending town hall meetings, or simply praying or holding positive intentions at home, no matter what they're doing they're simultaneously holding space for a resolution of the issue at hand. In times of great urgency, some of the wisdom keepers have served as activists on more controversial issues as well.

Thus far, this book has been mostly about the type of space holding we do by doing our personal growth work and healing individually, holding space for our dreams, holding space for those close to us, and holding space in professional settings. The art of entire groups of people holding space for the healing of certain issues is a powerful force in its own right, and though not the focus of this book, is entirely deserving of some mention. No matter how long it may take, we have seen results when large amounts of people tap into something greater and then hold space and intention for the healing and resolution of issues. Examples have been as large or small as ending slavery, granting women the right to vote, rescuing endangered and abused animals or people, changing unfair laws, protecting the earth's resources from destruction, or petitioning to free a wrongly accused person from prison. I advocate a microcosm-to-macrocosm approach to healing our society and believe that many of these issues would cease to exist if we were all more fully healed and whole on the inside. However, space holding for these issues in our current time is still a necessary pursuit. People are still exerting large amounts of peaceful energy attempting to right injustices every day and deserve to be recognized for their contributions to spaceholding. Though an activist's actions may be more noticeable by the greater populace, they are mostly being recognized for their doing and most people probably do not stop to think about all of the energy also expended into their being, while they intently hold space for the highest resolution for all involved.

If You Become a Parent

One of the Hardest Jobs as a Spaceholder—Parenting

A profession is not just something you get paid for doing. If you decide somewhere along your journey to share your world with a child or children, you will find that your spaceholding talents are essential to your job as a parent as well. However, you will probably quickly find that the considerations and techniques for holding space for adults are much different than holding space for children. In that case, you will definitely want to read the following…

Holding Space for Children is Different than Holding Space for Adults

All of the advice in this book thus far has applied to situations where one grown adult is holding space for either themselves, another grown adult, or a situation or conversation between themselves and another adult. When you, as an adult, hold space for a child, there are an entirely different set of circumstances to be considered.

First of all, a child is not an adult. Let me say that again, a child is not an adult. Even if they are a teenager, they are still not a fully grown adult. Some children may have you unconsciously believing they are little adults by the articulation, maturity, and responsibility that they display, but you must remember that they are still *not* adults. Children and teenagers spend their childhood learning, growing, and constantly changing, and in very different ways than adults. You may grow and change in your consciousness and beliefs as you continue to go through adulthood, but children are rapidly growing physically, mentally, and spiritually as they adopt all different stages of bodies, mental capacities, and visions of who they are.

If your child is not taking responsibility for or holding space for themselves if they are angry or distressed, you must remember as you respond to them that they are still learning how to cope with all of their physical, mental, emotional, and spiritual changes. They are still figuring out how to appropriately respond to their peers, adults, other

101

authority figures, and family as they are also developing their individuality. In many cases, society's emphasis on the masculine may also not be supporting them in developing this side of themselves. Your child may not be able to check themselves as easily as an adult can because they are still learning who they really are. Children and teenagers are constantly observing, mirroring, and imitating everything around them. They have not yet decided what they like, what they really feel, how to stay balanced, who they really are, or even who they want to be.

I will not delve further into the differences between a child and an adult, but will stress that your approach absolutely must be shifted appropriately and that no matter how smart, mature, or responsible the child may be, they are still a child, and they need you as their caregiver to constantly hold a safe space for them to grow and develop. A place of freedom, with proper boundaries and rules, and a space free from your own unhealed issues. Children need more boundaries than adults, but also need more allowances for their messy behaviors. They're still learning what is acceptable and what is not as they grow and change through all of the stages of childhood. Holding space for children requires extra patience, empathy, and attention than you may need to hold for adults. A child should not be held to the same standards as an adult and should, therefore, be treated differently. When you as an adult are in a position to hold space for a child, remember that it will look very different than when you hold space for yourself or another adult, and adjust yourself accordingly.

With this said, I want to stress that it is never fair or appropriate to ask (even energetically) your children to hold space for you, as that would be considered an upside-down relationship and would not be developmentally appropriate or healthy for the child . Any of your unhealed issues or traumas should be held in a space entirely separate from your relationship with them where they can be dealt with in an adult-like manner, by yourself, or with the help of other appropriate adults. Your children may have to deal with the same life situations as you do at certain times, but they should not be required to hold space for you as you process how to navigate these situations. You are the spaceholder for your children so they may be free to grow, develop, and uncover their own true selves, without the responsibility or burden of having to hold the space for you. Of course, as an adult, you'll have your own needs, emotions, or wounds that need attention. In those times, it is necessary to go only to your higher power, yourself, and other adults who are willing and capable of holding space for you so that you may heal separately and in a different space from the children or teenagers you are raising or caring for.

Be mindful as well not to judge, discipline, or respond to your children based on your own stressors or perceived faults. For example, if you want to punish your child for not getting their work done and at the same time you are frustrated and upset with yourself for not getting your work done, stop, take a breather, and hold space for yourself until you can assess the situation. Your child may, in fact, need discipline or consequences, but you'll need to separate your thoughts on those consequences from the discomfort you may be feeling about your own issues. Your actions may or may not have consequences for you as well, and they may or may not be considerable. Just remember that what is happening with your child is a separate issue and must be dealt with in a very different space than how the universe deals with you. So before you respond to what you need to in order to establish proper boundaries for your child, make sure that your own issues have been cleared out or put to the side and that you are dealing with them based on what *they* are doing or not doing, and nothing else. It is not okay for you, as a parent, to take out your frustrations of your own perceived shortcomings on your children (i.e. passing the poison) just because you're in a position of authority with them. As a caregiver, you should deal with them based on their own actions only and not allow your frustrations to cloud your decisions. Passing the poison is certainly damaging when done to adults, but taking out frustrations unjustly on children out of a lack of self-awareness, weariness, or due to being in a position of authority over them can provide even more devastating results to their psyches than to a grown adult. What you may want to instill or say to them out of frustration may become a booming voice in the back of their head that they'll have to deal with later in life in order to truly love themselves and thrive. This is not to imply that you should be perfect or punish yourself if you forget, but rather to speak to the type of awareness conscious parents who understand spaceholding would wish to cultivate. Just remember that your children are in a position of submissiveness and dependence on you until they are allowed to be on their own. You're a guide and caretaker of these evolving humans and will need to constantly remind yourself of the differences between them and other adults.

Conversely, there are also parents who put too much pressure on themselves and fail to give their children appropriate boundaries because they feel it unfair to administer consequences for the very same infractions they themselves are committing. If this sounds like you, take heart, know that you are their *consequence giver* at this time in their lives and that the universe will deal with you accordingly based on a host of other factors that you might not even know about. Using the previous example, as adults, there are many different things that come into play regarding whether or not you actually need to be getting your work done. Things like, did it actually need to get done by a certain deadline? Did it actually need to get done at all? Is this something you really dropped the ball on, or maybe the universe was guiding you away from putting any more energy into it, or you need to wait for a better time? The universe will also deal with you based on your deposits and withdrawals in all areas of your life and you cannot really attempt to factor those in when dealing with your children. You do not want to hold your children to higher standards than you are able to hold yourself, but you also need to recognize that they do need guidance and to learn the value of consequences while they are small, before life may deal out larger ones later on. It's still your job to do this no matter how hypocritical you may feel.

The last thing I want to mention is the children that you teach, love, and care for are your mirrors. They are often quietly learning, watching, and absorbing everything you do. Whenever they act up, always check yourself first to see if they are trying to show you something about yourself and then deal with them from there. You must take full responsibility for observing, owning, and processing your own feelings and emotions in all situations with others and *especially* those with your children, and then respond to them free of your own stressors. In many circumstances, dealing with your own issues that your children are mirroring for you, may just clear up your issues with them as well.

How Your Spaceholding Practices Can Affect the World

Congratulations, fellow traveler. You have learned how to identify yourself as a spaceholder, the value of intuition to your skill, how to take care of yourself before holding space for others, how to navigate personal relationships with your gift, how to use your talents in the creation process, how to manifest your dreams and goals, and how to use your talents professionally. Now you are about to discover how all of that self-reflection and personal growth affects not only you and those immediately around you but the entire world as well. Well done. You have become a peace builder and a change-maker for the universe just by working on yourself!

Making Yourself a Channel for Love and Peace—Be-ing Love

Adept spaceholders can actually affect the vibration of the mood and energy around them just by holding the authentic vibrations of love and peace. It is called creating a *resonant field*, or *coherence*. What they are *doing* is holding the frequency of *being* love. Now, contrary to some belief systems, you do not have to do anything specific to be love. In fact, that is exactly the point. *Being* love only requires that someone vibrate and hold the energy of love and peace in as many parts of their being as possible. There are many ways to be love and they do not all involve getting out there and *doing* something. There are different roles for different people at different times.

Sometimes a spaceholder is only required to hold space for themselves and those around them. Sometimes they are to teach and inspire, and other times they are to caregive. Sometimes, they are to write books and share them with the world. The way you will know which role is best for you is to check in with yourself and your divine helpers. Be sure that you are taking proper care of yourself as you hold the space for others and remember to start with the person in the mirror and the motto, "If you want to save the world, save yourself." Above all, living your life from the heart and based on love will inspire and affect all those around you, who will, in turn, affect all those around them.

So how do you get started on radiating love through just *being* love and holding the space for it? The answer may be different than you think. Tapping into feminine energy and increasing the effectiveness of your spaceholding can be achieved by clearing your inner vessel of past traumas, wounds, and old thoughts and beliefs that are no longer valid. Clearing your own blocks and barriers to love and freedom will allow for your being to more potently resonate with the frequency of love.

Please note, however, that this does not mean that you can just think about love and peace all of the time, and therefore hold the space for others, yourself, and the world. In order to become the clearest vessel and to radiate love, you must also be able to bring your darkest shadows to light in order to transmute them. Bringing balance to the duality of the world, including the duality inside of us, is one of the major tasks you will face in learning to be love. Holding the space for love involves exploring joy, pain, sorrow, strife, excitement, sadness, and fear. In a world of duality, we need to experience many of these in order to truly express our physicality and our spirituality. Love allows for you to feel your heart swell with pride or joy, or for it to break open into tiny pieces that yourself and others will have to love back into being in order for you to feel anything again. Love involves many different emotions such as despair, hope, trust, and surrender. Love involves being the best and deepest *us* we can be, without masks or suits of armor. Love can break us open, and love can set us free.

Due to the fact that spaceholders in general are always taking in, holding, transmuting, and clearing their individual and collective wounds, the path of *being love* may not always be pretty or without some tension and challenges on all sides. In other words, it can and will be messy and ugly at times. You would be wise in this case to remember that tough love, boundaries, and loving yourself are still love when those challenging times arise. In addition, remember to always breathe, center, and bring yourself back to love whenever you may find yourself moving away from it. A quick breath or two into your heart-center should be just enough to do the trick.

Becoming the Best Spaceholder That You Can Be

As you've read this book, you've learned what a valuable role spaceholding has in our society. You may have found that you have natural tendencies towards it, learned how to take care of yourself better while you do it, or that you would like to focus more of your energy on it. Here are some more solid tips on how to do that.

There are many ways to become a more proficient spaceholder. I've covered many of them briefly in different portions of this book. To really become a master, I would suggest that being attentive to and conscious of your own inner work and attending to your spiritual and personal growth, be placed at the top of your list. In order to best hold space for others and yourself, you'll need to be as clear a vessel as possible. A consistent stillness practice, regular contemplation of and strides toward your own personal growth, and time for rest and rejuvenation and fun, will help you tremendously.

To be a skilled spaceholder for others, professionally or otherwise, it is important that you can hold yourself tall and strong while also being kind and compassionate. You may think you have this leading and facilitating thing licked, but if there's any small part of you that doesn't believe in your ability or authority to hold the space for a group of people, the light will shine upon it so that you can strengthen and repair it. Be willing to swim in the deep end of your consciousness as a great spaceholder possesses the desire and willingness to do what I call *going there*. If you are not ready to go deep with your own triggers, blocks, and repeating unhealthy patterns, you will not be able to properly hold the space for others to go through and find theirs as well. To hold space, one must be able to cultivate or create a space in the first place. If you are not fully conscious, aware, and working through your own foibles, you will not have enough skill to know how to effectively pull back and open up the space to hold for yourself or others.

In doing your own work, one of the things you will learn is how to pull yourself out of a situation and to become an observer of yours and others' lives. Knowing how to take yourself out of the heart of situations and to see them from the standpoint of an observer is an important step towards holding space, lest you begin to take on other people's *stuff* that is not yours at all. If you haphazardly jump in to help others when you are not properly prepared for the rescue and skilled in how to keep yourself separate from them, you may find yourself drowning in emotions and feelings that aren't yours to sort out. Becoming an observer of your life also makes your issues less personal and will enable you to make clearer choices with less guilt about who and what you will spend your energy on. Again, spaceholding is an art and proficiency comes from practicing and fine tuning your craft while gaining the tools necessary to become a master of it.

In holding space for a group, professionally or otherwise, you will also need to be confident enough in yourself as the holder of that container to allow only what is highest and best to be brought into that space. In essence, you become unafraid to say no to things that don't belong in the space you are holding. If your talk or event has a specific topic but is an open discussion format, then your job will be to set the space and energetic boundaries for the space ahead of time, keep everyone on track, and to keep the space clear of anyone's intense emotions that don't belong in that space. Owning your power and being very present are two ways in which to do this. The more confident you are in yourself and your spaceholding abilities, the more healed you are, and the less you desire to worry about what others think of you, the more successful you will be. Please note, it is not necessary to be overly authoritative, controlling, or otherwise to make yourself look big and scary. You will be loving, but firm.

In order to do this, you'll need to love and approve of yourself and to work with anything that may keep you from feeling your true worth or value. This can be achieved by working with yourself on areas of your life where you may feel intimidated, less than, or unworthy, and figuring out why you feel that way. Once you've mastered this, and it will be an ongoing process, your very presence and the energy you carry will speak for themselves. Though you may still need to rein people in, as you respect yourself and the service you are providing to them by holding that space, they will respect your rules and boundaries for that space as well. In cases where they don't, you can have a polite conversation with them where you explain what behavior is acceptable within the space that you've set up. If they aren't in agreement with that, then it is just not a mutually agreeable situation, and hopefully you can respectfully part ways. If that doesn't work, you may need to ask them to leave.

Being a master spaceholder also means being as free as possible of judgment, both of yourself and others, and having an open-mind to whatever is coming up in the situation that space is being held for. In my duties as a wedding officiant, holistic life coach, and spiritual counselor, people respond the way they do to me because they can feel my genuine love and acceptance for who they are, what they believe in, where they are on their journey, and what tools they are using and experiences they are having. It is not for me to say what is best for them. My feeling is that as long as we're not hurting ourselves or others, we should be honored and accepted for whatever path guides us *home*.

Though it may seem that your work will be entirely in the feminine, that is not the case. You will also have to bolster your courage and motivation when action steps need to be taken. You may need to take some classes, do something, or get out and start talking to people. One cannot effectively clear their mind, body, and spirit by meditation and contemplation alone. Sometimes you will have to speak out, clear out, or otherwise take action toward moving yourself forward and keeping your energy clear and uncluttered. This is not to say that you can't have any noise or distraction around you, but just the opposite. The more you clear your energetic field, the more capable you'll be of walking into noisy situations without them affecting your energy. Anytime you're holding space for a gathering, event, or meeting, it's possible that people's emotions will bubble and rise to the surface. The point is, the better you get with owning your power and loving and respecting yourself, your time, your space, and your efforts and energy, the more often you'll bring to yourself pleasurable situations where everyone is respectful of the space you've created, as well as of you and the job you're doing as a spaceholder and facilitator.

EXAMPLES OF WHAT GOES ON BEHIND THE SCENES OF A PROFESSIONAL SPACEHOLDER

Spaceholding, teaching, or facilitating are careers where you will constantly need to be at your best. There is no room for relaxing into the space when you are the one charged with holding it by leading, facilitating, or keeping things on track. To a random guest at the weddings I officiate, it may seem that I don't have to be that *on* or that I don't really use that much energy in my ten to thirty minutes delivering a ceremony, but I most certainly do. This is why I can only do a few of them a day and why it's best that I usually have them scattered throughout the month, usually no more than two per weekend. Holding the energy for a crowd, especially when there's a lot of emotion coming up, takes a lot of focused presence from the spaceholder. Fortunately, at weddings most of the energy is joyful. However, even the intense energy of joy from a large group of people takes a lot to contain in even just half an hour of solemn focus of ceremonial rites on love and marriage. Though the energy is most often beautiful and lovely, I still need to do a good amount of grounding when I'm finished and must also shift myself a bit before I go on to another activity.

Another example is a small, intimate healing group I used to run as an extension of my coaching practice where there was no specific topic and the format was such that people were allowed to speak freely. I was not the leader exactly, but I was the facilitator. I told the group, as well as others who wanted to know about the group, that it was my job *to keep the car on the road*, so to speak. Every time we met, I would allow for small talk as everyone was getting there, but then would call the group to order when it was time for us to begin.

Being very tuned-in and energetically sensitive to the group, I would usually close my eyes for a minute and check in with how we should begin that day. The energy of where everyone was before we got there was always different and there was almost always an overriding theme I picked up for where we should begin that day and who needed what. Sometimes, I would intuit a jumping off topic while I was driving to our meeting spot. Other times, I would lead a short and always spontaneous guided meditation to relax and shift everyone into our space. Still other times, I might have heard something in the chatter of everyone arriving that I knew should be addressed right away. There were times when I would just look right at a person and ask them if they wanted to start. Of course, that person didn't necessarily want to share right away, but once they began to open up, we all usually realized the benefit of starting with them as what they had to say would usually be timely and healing for all of us.

Due to the fact that this was an open topic healing and sharing group, we were able to touch on anything that wanted to come out of the space and always have it be the right thing. In facilitating that group, I often felt like I was tending to a sacred fire. My job, in that case, was the fire-keeper, keeping it lit, burning and healthy, and then allowing whatever wisdom, knowledge, or healing that wanted to be born within the fire to touch all of us with its message.

Holding Space for All Humanity by Looking at Our Individual and Collective Shadows

In order to hold space for all humanity, you might begin to notice that the only thing you can really do is to work on yourself. What you also might begin to notice is that the only way humanity as a whole will change is if the majority of us transform on an individual level. Society has taught us that we must *make a* change from the outside-in or from the macrocosm to the microcosm, but really, it's the other way around. The collective heart cannot change until the majority of us have accepted both our light and our dark parts, and then made conscious choices about the behavior and actions we wish to display. When all of our aspects are recognized, and our actions are freely chosen, it is then that our individual transformations and new choices will begin to affect the collective heart, and we will all feel truly free. The macrocosm is truly just a reflection of our collective microcosms, in effect, the world on the outside that we see is a direct reflection of the world that lies inside of the majority of us.

Humans are inherently good people. It is mainly fear, trauma, unhealed wounds, and not accepting our shadowy parts that cause us to act out in unhealthy ways. Holding space for all of our feelings is of the utmost importance when attempting to turn these things around. Personal healing can affect planetary healing when we do our personal growth work to see where we hold all of those fears, traumas, wounds, and shadowy parts. Recall that in our individual and collective shadows lie all of the things that we judge ourselves for, feel ashamed of, or even those traits that we swear we don't have. Also, remember that our shadowy parts can also contain things that most people would deem as good or positive traits, but they are parts of ourselves that we've put away because either someone told us to, or we decided on our own were unacceptable.

When we do our personal growth work and are able to hold space for all of our feelings, they will not consume us to try to get our attention, and our shadow sides will not have to either go into hiding or come out in unhealthy ways. When we are either taught by others or believe ourselves that something we feel that we are is not okay, we'll judge ourselves or others for these things. When we judge others, many times we are merely making an outside judgment of something we cannot stand about ourselves, taking it off of us and projecting it onto a bystander where an *us and them* paradigm can continue to perpetuate. By removing the focus from ourselves and hyper-focusing on another person's faults or wrong choices, we have actually perpetuated darkness in our society by one more notch. We have now contributed to negativity, separation, and fear by augmenting the image of what a horribly wrong and poor choice the other has made, when in reality, we could be making the same choice in some aspect of ourselves.

Let's look at an easy example. If someone makes negative assumptions about another for their race, religion, socioeconomic status, or choice of who to love, they have now instituted fear and separation where it did not previously exist. Had that person looked at whatever was within themselves that may have caused their judgment of another, they could have seen an opportunity for transformation and love within themselves, therefore, willing inclusion and love, rather than separation, into the cosmos. If you imagine this happening in every individual heart every time someone goes to judge another or to project their unprocessed emotions outward, you can clearly see how much negativity, fear, and separation would be alleviated from entering into the collective heart on a daily basis. From the beginning, if we are able to hold space to work with the darkness in ourselves that exists without doing anything about it or judging others, we will no longer be passing the poison and can surely affect the greater macrocosm in a more harmonious way.

When our judgments are just feelings, we can hold the space to work with them while we are feeling them, and allow them to come out of the darkness and into the light in a safe space for healing and release. Although we may be disgusted with ourselves for having a negative thought or judgment against another, we can instead hold space for that darkness to show itself to us and shed some light on why we may feel that way. That darkness is simply looking to be acknowledged. The more we shove it away, the more it will continue to come out of us in unhealthy ways. Remember that our healthy and positive traits that we've put into our shadow want very much to come back front and center and to help us really shine as we give our true gifts to the world.

Holding space for all humanity begins with each one of us becoming conscious of our own light and dark sides and then making choices based on love instead of fear. And of course, believing in ourselves and humanity and that a world of love, harmony, and inclusion is absolutely possible. Or, as Gandhi put it, "Be the change you wish to see in the world." When every person begins to have the courage to look at all of the lessons and opportunities for choice or action that life has given them, the whole of society cannot help but to move forward in a more positive direction.

Holding Space for Growth and Change in Romantic Partnerships and Friendships,
And How This Can Affect the Healing of the Entire Planet

You can hold space, grow, and change either alone—by reading, writing, meditating, going to workshops—or you can do it within a romantic partnership or friendship. Our partners can provide us with our biggest mirrors to areas in ourselves that need growth. The more supportive the partner, the faster and more exponentially we can grow.

There is no way to run from our stuff when we're in an intimate relationship. It will continue to show up for us within the relationship until we agree to look at and work with it. When we come to the table every day within our relationships, we begin to recognize that these situations and perceived issues are actually wonderful opportunities to grow and heal our wounds. Healing our individual wounds on this level increases the healing throughout the greater universe. When each of us individually grows, changes, and heals our wounds, our collective wounds begin to heal as well, and the collective world's biggest wound, the wound of separateness, can begin to be faced head on.

Through healthy, evolved partnerships and more respectful and loving relationships, we can begin to learn that there is no *other* and no *enemy* to fight. When we recognize our stuff through the loving eyes and hearts of our intimate partners, we no longer feel separate and alone. We will no longer see *us and them out there* on the greater stage. We will begin to see that the world out there is really just a reflection of all of our worlds *in here*, and we'll begin to see a real change in global healing on a massive scale. Our commitment and love towards our partners can give us the motivation to affect the greater consciousness through our willingness to grow and evolve within our partnerships, therefore lifting the world around us as well.

No matter what our story, above all else we all desire to love and be loved. I believe that if we heal the wounds within ourselves first, and then within our partnerships, families, and communities, this is how we will eventually bring about the global peace and harmony that we wish to see. This is true *transformation* from the inside out, not merely *change* from the outside in. When we can do this within ourselves, our intimate relationships will be healthier. When our intimate relationships are healthier, our families will be healthier. When our families are healthier, our communities will be healthier. It is of the utmost importance to first heal ourselves, then our relationships, our families, our communities, our world, and our universe. If we attempt to change the world without this foundational healing and attempt to re-build on a wounded separateness consciousness, we are again building our houses on sand.

Conclusion

Why Holding Space is Important to Transforming the World

A few years ago, I wasn't so sure I agreed with the value of holding space and transforming ourselves on an individual level in order to bring about the peace and harmony we wished to see in the world. I didn't understand how we could just sit around *working on ourselves* and not really *doing* anything to help all of the situations in our world that clearly needed as much help as they could get. Who were we to sit in our homes and meditate while things seemed to be just getting worse? And why weren't those of us who were doing well enough for ourselves consistently helping the poor, the abused, the meek, and the downtrodden? How was each of us doing our inner work going to reverse all of the evil and unfairness that was running rampant in our world?

When I first became a holistic life coach, I owned a holistic wellness center. At one point I began to ask my clients to help me with food and clothing drives that I was setting up for people I had found who needed help. I figured if we were so privileged, why weren't we *doing* something? I was told by a man that I knew that I was using my energy in the wrong direction, that I should have been using more of my energy towards those with money and clout, the *movers and the shakers*, and offer my services to them. I didn't see how doing that would satisfy me, or how I could reconcile it within myself that I was flirting with the *big boys and girls* rather than keeping my humble feet on the ground.

After a while, it became clear that this was just old programming, part of what has kept many of us from living more fruitful lives. How can any of us thrive if none of us allow ourselves to thrive and if we all strive to stay small and *not* prosper? After a few more years, a few more experiences, and a little reflection, I also realized that as of right now, these movers and shakers are the ones making the decisions that shape the lives of everyone else. If these people aren't feeling good about themselves, or if they have a bone to pick with someone or a personal vendetta to settle, that was inevitably going to come out in their public policies and rules and laws for us all to live by. Their rules and laws affect all sorts of things and play a major role in the general shaping of a culture and society. So if my goal is to empower people and to help create a world of cooperation, joy, peace, and harmony, why wouldn't I want to be among the movers and the shakers who are most able to influence the structures of our society? After all, they are the ones making it easier or harder for all of us to grow into our true selves, cooperate with each other and thrive.

This doesn't mean that I don't help people when I feel guided, it's just that I'm guided more by compassion now and not as much by empathy or charity, which is not as bad a thing as I may have originally thought. It certainly keeps my cup fuller so I have more to give out to the world in the ways that I uniquely can.

These days many more people are beginning to awaken to their true spiritual nature. Those of us in more economically and socially stable countries tend to have more time, energy, and resources to cultivate a spiritual and stillness practice. We can tip the scales of humanity on behalf of ourselves and others who are either not able to or have a different calling at this time. If you have awakened and feel the fire burning within you to delve into yourself, then know that we need you. If you feel without a doubt that this is what you must do, you will undoubtedly affect and inspire those around you with the life choices and decisions that you make that are born out of the higher field of love, cooperation, and joy that is cultivated through your space holding and personal growth practice. Although there is still reason to help out where you can and when your energy feels aligned, a large part of your biggest job right now is to affect the collective by transforming yourself. Once you've done that, share what you have gained and learned. Your individual transformation, born within the feminine container of holding space, can have a giant effect on the world at large when you then bring the creations that you bore into the world through the masculine energy.

The days of some people being disempowered and others rushing in to save them is fading fast. It's time for us all to stand up and take responsibility for the world we would like to live in. Our goal now is to empower ourselves, and then each other, raising us all into the best versions of ourselves that we can be. Ironically enough, this standing up may involve *slowing down* enough to figure out who we really are, living our lives out loud, inspiring those around us, and ultimately slowly changing the way the world is set up. Our collective consciousness is what causes things to go one way or the other. If enough of us can wake up to our true and authentic selves by getting still and quiet and doing our personal work, we will live outside of the perceived parameters of current society. When more and more of us can do that, society at large changes. It has to. The tipping point will have no other place to go than where the masses direct it to go. Therefore, I write this book to you, to help you understand what it means to hold space and to ask you to love and honor yourself for doing it. Although you may think you're not *doing* anything, you just might be saving the world by being your authentic and full self. The self you found in the quiet and stillness of **Holding Space**.

About the Author

Amanda (meaning "worthy of love") Dobra Hope has gone on a life journey true to her name. Possessing a strong knowledge of the wisdom she carried inside to see and know higher truth, combined with an insatiable searching for that truth, she has been led to many interesting modalities, people, and places. Ultimately, however, her journey was not to outside things, but an inner journey to strengthen her love and belief in herself and her talents, leading her to share that wisdom with the world. She is passionate about helping people to learn and practice personal responsibility, personal growth, and higher spiritual truth in order to merge their spiritual and physical worlds together. Her belief is that when everyone on the planet sees themselves as both a spiritual and physical being, loves themselves, and can express their true gifts with passion and authenticity, we will all thrive. Amanda holds a Doctorate in Holistic Life Coaching, a Master of Divinity in Metaphysics, and various certifications in other holistic modalities. Born in Wisconsin, with a brief residence in Hawaii, she now lives in the rolling hills of Nashville, TN where she serves as a holistic life coach, author, speaker, and wedding officiant.

ALL THINGS THAT MATTER PRESS

FOR MORE INFORMATION ON TITLES AVAILABLE FROM
ALL THINGS THAT MATTER PRESS, GO TO
http://allthingsthatmatterpress.com
or contact us at
allthingsthatmatterpress@gmail.com

If you enjoyed this book, please post a review on Amazon.com and
your favorite social media sites.
Thank you!

Printed in Great Britain
by Amazon